# SPARKING LEARNING in YOUNG CHILDREN

## Classroom Best Practices

### Chris Amirault, Ph.D.

## Publishing Credits

Corinne Burton, M.A.Ed., *President* and *Publisher*
Aubrie Nielsen, M.S.Ed., *EVP of Content Development*
Kyra Ostendorf, M.Ed., *Publisher, professional books*
Véronique Bos, *Vice President of Creative*
Cathy Hernandez, *Senior Content Manager*
Courtenay Fletcher, *Cover Designer*

## Image Credits

All images from Shutterstock

## Library of Congress Cataloging-in-Publication Data

Names: Amirault, Chris, author.
Title: Sparking learning in young children : classroom best practices / Chris Amirault.
Description: Huntington Beach, CA : Shell Educational Publishing, Inc, [2025] | Includes bibliographical references and index. | Summary: "Transform early childhood learning with expert guidance for inclusive and developmentally appropriate teaching in your classroom"-- Provided by publisher.
Identifiers: LCCN 2024005184 (print) | LCCN 2024005185 (ebook) | ISBN 9798765971956 (paperback) | ISBN 9798765971970 (epub) | ISBN 9798765971963 (ebook)
Subjects: LCSH: Early childhood education. | Early childhood education--Curricula. | Motivation in education. | Child development. | Classroom environment. | BISAC: EDUCATION / Schools / Levels / Early Childhood (incl. Preschool & Kindergarten) | EDUCATION / Professional Development
Classification: LCC LB1139.23 .A67 2025 (print) | LCC LB1139.23 (ebook) | DDC 372.21--dc23/eng/20240411
LC record available at https://lccn.loc.gov/2024005184
LC ebook record available at https://lccn.loc.gov/2024005185

**Shell Education**

A division of Teacher Created Materials
5482 Argosy Avenue
Huntington Beach, CA 92649-1039
**www.tcmpub.com/shell-education**
**ISBN 979-8-7659-7195-6**
© 2025 Shell Educational Publishing, Inc.

# Table of Contents

# Introduction

*Sparking Learning in Young Children* provides educators an overview of what they need to know to get started in a preschool or preK classroom. The following chapters introduce crucial topics in early childhood education (ECE). The insights here are drawn from recent research, best practices, and firsthand experience. And they're delivered with good humor and lively energy, so that you can spark learning not only in children, but also in yourself!

This book does not tell you which curriculum and assessments to use. And it is not a "how to teach" guide. Rather, it serves to set teachers up for success. Whether you're in your first year teaching young children or you're an experienced teacher, this book will guide, support, and encourage you so you can help all children in your classroom start their educational journeys with delight and confidence.

In this book, the terms *young children* and *preschoolers* both refer to children between the ages of three and five. (However, nearly everything here applies to working with all students under age five or six.) *Preschool* is the general term for programs for preschoolers, whether they take place in a district building or an early childhood education program. *PreK* refers to programs that serve three- and four-year-old children. Several states offer universal, publicly funded programs for four-year-old children. These programs are known by various names, including *transitional kindergarten (TK), voluntary preKindergarten (VPK),* and *preK.*

## Overview

The first chapter focuses on **child development**, the critical foundation of the ECE field. The science of child development has grown significantly in the last several years. This knowledge helps us better understand the relationships between social expectations, culture and identity, brain and body development, and difficult experiences. Many of the basic insights you bring to your work will be affirmed. Others may be questioned or expanded. Exploring child development in depth is the foundation for everything else the book covers.

Chapter 2 is about **planning and reflection**. One key research insight is that children benefit from a very particular balance. They need set, expected routines and structure. But they also need free play, new materials and experiences, and emergent, responsive activities. That balancing act requires educators to learn how to work as a team to plan routine tasks, child experiences, and the flow of the day. To spark true learning, you need thoughtful, respectful planning and reflection in all you do. This mindset allows you to support children's development as individuals and as part of the classroom community. It also creates a more enjoyable, empowering professional experience for you!

Chapter 3 considers **room design and materials**. This chapter repeatedly asks the same two questions: Who is this object or material for? How is it used? Too often classrooms are designed for adults, with lots of commercial products and sensory noise. Overwhelming learning environments have little educational purpose—and they drain precious teacher funds! The chapter starts with the critical areas of safety and health. It then explores ways to find the sweet spot, with just enough engaging spaces and materials to spark learning throughout the day.

Chapter 4 focuses on creating powerful **curriculum, assessment, and instruction cycles**. Let's face it: sometimes curriculum can feel like an imposition, making instruction feel robotic. Assessment often seems like tedious paperwork. But our profession provides us with extraordinary opportunities. We are not required to follow a thick textbook, relentlessly covering all of the content. Instead, we get to focus on children and development. We determine what children know and can do, and we are part of the powerful moments that help them take their next steps. This chapter establishes simple and effective ways to approach these cycles. We can support everyone in the classroom, being accountable to both our program's administrative requirements and the ever-changing children we serve!

Chapter 5 dives into **family engagement**, tying the ideas from previous chapters into an overall approach for working with families. Parents and caregivers see and understand things about their children that they can share with you. This can help you create engaging environments for every child. At the same time, most ECE teachers are important members of their communities. They provide families with education and care for children. This chapter shares new research on family engagement and helps you build ongoing, meaningful relationships with families.

Throughout each chapter, you'll see text boxes that suggest additional resources to spark your learning. These are for you to use as you bring the topics in the book to life. You can explore a given topic in greater depth online, in print, or as part of a professional dialogue.

# The Ten Key Principles for Preschool Classroom Design

As an early childhood school director for the last two decades, I've learned that there is one thing that all strong educators share: they create classrooms and schools driven by clearly stated, deeply held principles that they return to over and over in every aspect of their work. These principles aren't window dressing. Rather, they are living, breathing mindsets that are important when establishing relationships, norms, and communities. And they are especially critical in challenging times, providing guidance when the path forward is less than clear.

So, here in *Sparking Learning in Young Children*, we'll do just that, using the following ten principles. (Feel free to edit these or to add your own!)

### Remember: Education Is Care, and Care Is Education

Our field has debated its name for decades, but one thing current research tells us over and over is that terrific early childhood education is grounded in an ethic of care. Outstanding care for children is the only way to provide them with the education that they deserve. The two go hand in hand!

### Make Every Interaction Matter (Because Every Interaction Matters)

Early childhood education is based on strong, consistent, nurturing relationships. These relationships are between children and teachers, between teachers and families, and between children themselves. Relationships are built one interaction at a time, so we strive to make every interaction matter. And when something goes awry, we reflect on that interaction to rebuild the relationship. Infant mental health professionals call this "the cycle of rupture and repair."

## Prioritize Honesty, Transparency, and Trust with Everyone

It's not always easy to say the truth, the whole truth, and nothing but the truth! But in early childhood education, it's critical to practice honesty and transparency as much as possible. Our entire field is built on the expectations that parents trust us with their most precious family members and that children trust us as well. Honesty and transparency are the two communication essentials for building that trust.

**3**

## Keep Your Equity Lens Handy

Recognizing and honoring the diversity of each child, adult, family, and community member in your classroom is essential. It is the right thing to do all the time, not once in a while or at special events. This commitment is the only way to provide both outstanding educational experiences and truly responsive care. Being equitable means addressing inequalities that result in advantages for some and disadvantages for others. We now know that equity is essential for outstanding learning environments. We all have our biases and blind spots, so we must grab that equity lens regularly to explore situations—and ourselves.

**4**

## Design and Plan for Every Child and Family

This principle guides you to make decisions that balance group and individual needs. You'll need your equity lens in hand. At times, you'll prioritize a child with behavioral challenges or a family struggling with preschool routines. When you do, watch out for the misunderstanding that "it isn't fair." Remember that in early childhood (and probably in life!), everyone is working on something. Our classrooms are often the last chance children and families have to learn what they need for the K–12 world ahead!

**5**

## Do Your Best with What You've Got

At times, you may feel like your work is demanding too much of you. It may seem daunting to consider implementing all the ideas in this book. But let's face it: no one works in a perfect setting. We all have to deal with financial constraints, challenging situations, and imperfect humans (including ourselves!). So instead of jumping into the blame game, assess your resources, prioritize your strengths, and cut yourself some slack. Just do your best.

**6**

## Celebrate Successes and Rethink Flops

Establishing the right mindset for a great classroom environment is critical. Celebrate the many daily successes with the team, children, and families, and devote time to reflecting on the snafus. We'll never be perfect! But we can create a positive approach that elevates the good stuff and rethinks the not-so-good stuff.

**7**

## Lead with Collaboration and Communication

"You can't do it alone, but no one can do it for you." This well-known saying also applies to the early childhood classroom! No matter our role, we can lead by collaborating with other educators, with family members, and with the children themselves. That often requires asking lots of questions instead of pronouncing lots of opinions, and seeking out those who don't feel their voices matter.

**8**

### Move from Compliance to Ownership

Let's face it: even though we work in the most important profession on the planet, it often feels like we don't get a whole lot of respect. That attitude can make the expectations of our profession feel burdensome. We have to think of district mandates, corporate requirements, quality rating systems, state licensing, and more. When these demands feel like a burden, try hard to move from compliance to ownership. Find ways to make those expectations meaningful for the children and families you serve, as well as your colleagues. This won't make the challenges disappear, but learning how to make them useful is an invaluable leadership skill.

### When in Doubt, Take a Look from a Child's Perspective

Finally, whenever things get difficult, take a moment to change your position—literally! Sit on a child's chair or on the floor. Look at the situation from the perspective of the children in your care. What do things look like at the three- to four-foot height? What might be happening in children's bodies and brains? Putting the child at the center of our situation often makes the difficult things less challenging and makes our responses to them more thoughtful and compassionate.

## Your Story as a Professional Educator and Caregiver

As you can see from this introduction, this book is nothing without you. It is utterly meaningless unless you can find a way to connect what you read here to your own journey as an educator and caregiver. So I urge you to take a moment (or more) for reflection before diving in.

Set down the book, pick up a pen and paper, and respond to this prompt:

> *What expertise, knowledge, and insight can you bring to children, colleagues, and families as an early childhood professional right now? What expertise, knowledge, and insight would help you serve them better? What learning story do you want to tell about yourself on your journey to become the best educator and caregiver you can be?*

I share similar reflective questions at the end of each chapter to help you make the content become part of your own story.

After two decades in early childhood education—running programs, providing trainings, serving on state and national committees, teaching in higher education, and writing articles and books—I've learned that the best educators never reach the end of their learning journey. We just keep walking on our paths together, gathering sparks of inspiration as we go.

I hope that *Sparking Learning in Young Children* will help you on that journey. I can't wait!

# CHAPTER 1

# Child Development

Child growth and development is a complex, fascinating dance of interactions between the child, other people, the child's experiences, their environments, and much more. Children exist not in isolation but in profound connection to all that is around them. This connection is literally a matter of life and death to newborns, and it remains essential to development throughout childhood. This is why we stress the importance, in principle 2, of making every interaction matter—because every interaction matters.

Despite their need for caregivers, children are born with the ability and intent to extend their physical, cognitive, language, social, and emotional development. Infants move their heads toward sounds, reach out to grab their feet or a toy, and communicate with others using facial expressions and nonverbal utterances. Preschoolers roll on the ground, test caregiver limits for acceptable behavior, stack objects and knock them over, and get into and resolve disputes with their peers. All of this happens without any adult telling them what to do. Their brains and bodies are actively exploring the world.

With this understanding of child development, early childhood educators seek to activate children's exploration and learning through *play*. Play is not a simple thing! Rather, it is a complex web of ongoing interaction that forms the basis for how children develop. As Mr. (Fred) Rogers said, recalling Jean Piaget and Maria Montessori, "Play is often talked about as if it were a relief from serious learning. But for children, play is serious learning."

Play involves so many vital skills that it's impossible to name them all. Play includes complex thinking and problem-solving, self-regulation and persistence, physical adaptation to environments and situations, and communication skills including (but not limited to) language development. All of these are regular parts of preschool play. And, as our first principle reminds us, all this playful learning takes place within inclusive, caring, supportive relationships.

As teachers, we need to create those thoughtful relationships that support such play by repeatedly using this three-step process (discussed in greater detail in chapter 4):

1. We observe children at play to learn about their developmental strengths and needs. We try to understand what we see through the child's perspective.

2. We compare our observations to our knowledge of child development, noting those strengths and needs while guided by research.

3. We provide positive support both for a child's strengths and successes and for their next developmental steps, a process we refer to as *scaffolding*.

Here's an example. You notice that a child wearing a construction hat and safety vest is standing outside the block area, watching two other similarly dressed children build a road with blocks (1). You recall that several children are learning the critical social skill of entering into play (2). So you kneel down beside the child and say, "It looks like you're dressed to enter the construction zone! Shall we ask these two kids how you can participate?" (3). Slowly edging into the area, you encourage the child to ask what they can do, and the play unfolds from there.

This process of paying close attention to children and using your knowledge of child development to plan experiences that help them learn and grow is something you do every day, maybe without even realizing it! But being intentional with the process will help ensure that you're sparking learning throughout the day in the most appropriate ways possible. Activating your understanding of child development will help you do this. Personally, I find it to be the glorious, beating heart of all we do—and I enjoy it so much I do it whenever a young child is around!

## Developmentally Appropriate Practice

The key to this process is *developmentally appropriate practice*, or DAP (NAEYC 2020). The most recent statement from the National Association for the Education of Young Children (NAEYC) on DAP stresses three core considerations when supporting young children's learning and growth.

**TO SPARK YOUR LEARNING...** NAEYC released its original position statement on developmentally appropriate practice in the mid-1980s and has been updating it regularly ever since. In 2020, following work on current research that explicitly addresses equity concerns, NAEYC released its most recent position statement in coordination with a new position statement on equity (see page 12). Read the 2020 DAP position statement at naeyc.org/resources/position-statements/dap.

## Commonality

The first core consideration of DAP is *commonality*. Commonality refers to those aspects of child development that nearly all children commonly share. It seems simple enough! But because of the complicated history of our field, we need to proceed with some caution.

As educators in the twenty-first century, we have access to a wide range of insights about child development that are the result of many years of research. That research reaffirms our belief in the foundational importance of early child development. We now know a lot about the common features of development throughout early childhood. And we have a lot of guidance about how to support each of those areas of development for all children.

But this is where we need to be careful. These common features of development are not the same as developmental norms. Developmental norms are benchmarks used to determine whether a child is "ahead of the curve" or "falling behind." Indeed, one major research insight is that norms can be dangerous, even harmful, to children and the adults who care for them.

For example, one feature of child development is variability. Children develop at different speeds. Their bodies invest energy in one area while another area may be developing more slowly or even slipping back a bit. A child who had been sleeping through the night and is now learning to use the toilet regularly might regress and begin to wake up in the night. Put differently, the research tells us that children operate on their own developmental timelines. Labeling a child as "advanced" or "behind" misses a fundamental truth about child development.

As a result, there is no one way that all children develop across this commonly held set of developmental steps. Children do eventually learn to sleep through the night *and* use the toilet. We understand the common developmental expectations, which are explored in detail later in this chapter. But we hold them lightly, recognizing that each child is unique and develops uniquely.

## Individuality

Thus, the second core consideration of DAP is *individuality*, the unique characteristics of each child. Individuality is simply another way to embrace principle 10—always placing the child's perspective at the center of our consideration. It's our sustained commitment: to find and recognize each child within a commonly shared foundation. Based on that recognition, we create experiences that help them learn and grow.

The most valuable and engaging experiences we can create for children take their whole world into account. As NAEYC states, "Early childhood educators have the responsibility of getting to know each child well, understanding each child as an individual and as a family and community member. . . . Educators understand that each child reflects a complex mosaic of knowledge and experiences" (NAEYC 2021, xxxi).

## Context

Within developmentally appropriate practice, this complex mosaic is referred to as *context*. This is the third core consideration of DAP. Individuals are never alone! They are always embedded in multiple environments, relationships, and systems. NAEYC defines context as "everything discernible about the social and cultural contexts for each child, each educator, and the program as a whole" (NAEYC 2021, xxxi). *Everything* really does mean everything! That's why a good early childhood educator forms deep, meaningful relationships with the families and communities of the children they serve (principle 5). Families are key to understanding young children's contexts.

# Activating Your Equity Lens

When NAEYC revised their position statement on DAP in 2020, the consideration of context was greatly expanded. It takes into account the latest research about how children learn and grow. That research points not only to the child's context but also to our own as early childhood educators.

> An equity lens is a particular way of seeing the design and implementation of everything we do as educators. Our equity lens helps us pay special attention to the ways that some people might be served, for better or worse, by our actions.

We bring our own histories, experiences, values, and meanings into everything we do. That's particularly true for our work as early childhood educators; we operate within larger social, racial, economic, historical, and political contexts that impact us as well. We work in relentlessly social environments. We must bring all of our selves into dialogue with everyone and everything we encounter.

These personal contexts are intertwined and dynamic. They change and interact at each moment, and they shape and are shaped by our ongoing interactions with others and the world. Each decision we make with children, families, our colleagues, and ourselves can have a profound impact on the contexts that mean the most to us. That's why we embrace principle 2: every interaction matters.

The research on learning and context required NAEYC to rethink the relationship between equity and developmentally appropriate practice. We now understand that DAP and equity are intimately related—inseparable, in fact! As a result, principle 4's equity lens is applied to these three considerations of commonality, individuality, and context throughout this book.

An equity lens is a particular way of seeing the design and implementation of everything we do as educators. Our equity lens helps us pay special attention to the ways that some people might be served, for better or worse, by our actions. This attention enables us to identify and reduce or eliminate barriers. In that way, we can create more equitable experiences and environments for all children and families.

## Commonality through an Equity Lens

The idea of commonality is informed by shared insights drawn from the research base about how young children develop. Sounds simple, right? But this seemingly basic idea, when viewed through an equity lens, can reveal serious consequences. As it turns out, much of the knowledge base in early childhood is based on research that—when reexamined through an equity lens—is indeed *not* universally shared but rather is culturally specific.

For example, many of us have been taught that attachment is a universally held fact of child development. In our work, given the importance of caring relationships with children, we bring our own assumptions about positive attachment practices to everything we do. The very notion of "caring relationships" has attachment at the center! However, we now know that attachment practices can vary widely by culture and experience. The way each of us understands attachment is not now and never has been a universal norm.

Similarly, we prioritize play as a central tenet of our field. However, many educators assume that "play" has a single definition with particular values related to rules, safety, child autonomy, and so on. But play provides children with opportunities to engage with, interpret, explore, and make sense of their environments. And each of those environments is shaped by intersecting social and cultural contexts that differ among us.

Here's an example: For many years, I facilitated a family workshop devoted to outdoor play. I would ask the parents and caregivers to close their eyes and take a minute to imagine outdoor play when they were children. I then asked them to open their eyes and look around the room. Invariably, they would see that everyone else was smiling as they reminisced about these joyous times.

Then, everyone would share some descriptions of their outdoor play. This was always fascinating. These descriptions made it very clear that people had radically different notions of joy, risk, independence, order, and so on. It all depended on the context. Some people described adult-organized athletic events. Others described impromptu games that children created collaboratively on the spot. One person explained why their parents only allowed them to go outside if they were supervised. Others were allowed unsupervised play for hours and told to "come back before it gets dark."

It was an experience that allowed the group to see the importance of approaching a seemingly simple concept like play with care and nuance. At the start of the workshop, no one knew that they had deeply held biases about something as simple as play. This exercise made it clear that, in fact, we all do!

The biases related to attachment, play, and many other key elements of our field have had real human consequences over the years. As NAEYC states, "Differences from this Western (typically White, middle-class, monolingual English-speaking) norm have been viewed as deficits, helping to perpetuate systems of power and privilege and to maintain structural inequities" (NAEYC 2021, xxx–xxxi). Let's unpack that dense statement a bit with a personal example, similar to the one described in the play workshop above.

Perhaps you have experienced judgment of your family or your parenting as inadequate based on a norm that didn't really fit you or your child. Most people learn at an early age that their family's routines, habits, and environments aren't true for everyone. Breakfast, lunch, and dinner can involve a wide range and variety of foods, seating (or standing!) arrangements, preparations, and so on. That makes sense to us as adults. But when you first learn that not everyone eats a certain meal at dinnertime, it can come as a shock!

Unfortunately, those differences sometimes become judgments. You may have had experiences where that was the case. Maybe you felt that your clothes weren't as "nice" as those of other children. Or maybe you were teased for the food in your lunch box. If so, then you know what can happen when differences become norms, judgments that are used to privilege some things at the expense of others. Let's be clear—we all do this to a certain extent! It's nearly impossible not to standardize aspects of life. It's how you respond to so-called differences that matters.

When we review our approaches to early childhood education with an equity lens, we see that child development can never be based on universal norms, despite our understandable human assumptions otherwise. For that reason, we must use our equity lenses on a regular basis in order to recognize these biases as a result of our own experiences. By doing this repeatedly, we can see how certain notions of child development may benefit some children and constrain others. These efforts enable us to make the changes we need to truly serve all children.

As the examples above make clear, we need to apply an equity lens to the individuality of each student and to our own individuality as well. We work in a field that requires serious reflection on who we are. That means working to recognize what our biases are and how they shape what we see and don't see, what we recognize and value, and what we ignore or devalue.

So, to do this job with our equity lens in hand, we need to do the challenging work of recognizing our own experiences and contexts, which we bring into our work (principle 3). Our commitments to children require us to be as transparent with ourselves as possible about our biases and blind spots. We trust that doing so will lead to better experiences for children and families and more rewarding professional experiences for ourselves.

> We work in a field that requires serious reflection on who we are. That means working to recognize what our biases are and how they shape what we see and don't see, what we recognize and value, and what we ignore or devalue.

And we need to do our best with what we've got (principle 6). I've got myself, you've got yourself, and we're stuck with both! So with humility, diligence, and a sense of humor, let's commit to getting to know ourselves as best we can. This will enable us to use those selves in the most powerful, equitable way possible.

When we combine a deeper understanding of the children we serve and the individuals we are, we can build better contexts for children, families, and ourselves. And because we and they are always growing and developing, we need to keep our equity lens out all the time.

TO SPARK YOUR LEARNING... The 2019 NAEYC position statement "Advancing Equity in Early Childhood Education" was a landmark document that described the research basis for, core principles of, and recommendations proceeding from a deep commitment to providing equitable opportunities for every child. Read the full statement at naeyc.org/resources/position-statements/equity.

## Jumping to Judgment and Felina's Story

The rest of this chapter provides a basic overview of the four areas of development—physical, cognitive, language and literacy, social and emotional—we typically use in early childhood education, presenting important developmental frameworks and definitions for each. They overlap significantly, so you'll see aspects of each area shown in other areas when the overlap is most meaningful. Following these overviews, you'll find special issues to consider as you prepare your classroom. These sections highlight topics of particular interest given recent research and practice.

As you read, keep in mind that these overviews of child development require you to use the three core DAP considerations of commonality, individuality, and context. And always keep your equity lens at the ready. In particular, remember the warning about universal norms: *these overviews are not checklists used to judge children's development!*

One last, important point, which I can illustrate with a humiliating story. Early in my career as a preschool director, my favorite teacher (yes, I had a favorite) and I were faced with a complicated challenge. We had a student who, at the start of the school year, was acting like a cat. Felina (not her real name!) meowed and purred; she would cuddle up next to the other students, prompting them to pet her and bring her things to play with. She didn't speak and, like a proper cat, completely ignored adult instructions. For the first few weeks, she was basically the class pet.

The teacher and I were flummoxed. When we researched this sort of behavior, we saw all sorts of scary warnings about child development. Concerned that Felina had major delays, we became convinced that we needed to meet with the parent as soon as possible.

It turned out to be one of the most important family meetings I ever had—but not for the reasons I anticipated. We sat down with the parent and, very delicately, began sharing our concerns with her. We were trying not to alarm her as we had grown alarmed. We expected her to grow increasingly troubled, but instead she started smiling and shaking her head. When we were done presenting our concerns, the mom said, "Look, she is playing you." Our mouths flew open; we were shocked.

The mom then told us the following story. The previous night after dinner, Felina had asked Mom to give her some cookies that were out of her reach, on the top shelf of the cupboard. Mom said no, and then she went into another room to finish folding the laundry.

When she came back into the kitchen, her daughter was sitting at the kitchen table enjoying a snack of milk and cookies. Mom crossly asked her what happened. Felina had grabbed a kitchen chair and pushed it up to the counter. She then climbed up the chair to stand on the counter, reached up to the top shelf of the cupboard, and got the box of cookies. She got down and pushed the chair back to the kitchen table. She then got herself a glass from another shelf and the milk from the refrigerator, and poured herself a glass of milk. Felina somewhat sheepishly retold the entire sequence, though of course with a little bit of preschooler pride.

In short, her daughter had demonstrated clear skill in basically every area of development (with the possible exception of parental compliance!). Her motor development was outstanding, she had the ability to make a multistep plan and execute it perfectly, and she could retell that plan in detail. And though she ignored her mom's instructions, she certainly understood that she was violating them given the look on her face when her mom caught her red-handed.

And as for that whole cat business? Mom had seen it before at large family gatherings: it was her sophisticated way to read the room and get a whole bunch of people to treat her like their precious furry friend. Mom was right. Felina was playing us.

Felina and her mom taught us one of the most important lessons for preschool educators: *all behavior is situational.* As a result, statements about what a child "can" and "can't" do are very dangerous. Such statements interpret specific behaviors in specific situations as defining markers of a child's abilities.

**TO SPARK YOUR LEARNING...** I want to point out a serious flaw in the way that the teacher and I handled the situation with Felina. I wrote that "we researched this sort of behavior." Our haphazard, careless approach to assessing a child's challenges is an extremely dangerous practice. I often hear this creeping into discussions about children's development. Determining a child's disability status is a complicated process that can lead to very significant consequences for the child and family. As such, it's a job for experts in your school and district. Contact them with any concerns you have, and resist making your own diagnosis at all costs. A full exploration of this complex topic is beyond the scope of this book. For more information, I recommend Pamela Brillante's book *The Essentials: Supporting Young Children with Disabilities in the Classroom* (2017) as a great place to start your journey.

Nearly all the behaviors we observe in the children we work with happen in classroom situations outside of their usual home environments. Given those differences in location, we need to understand all of a child's behavior as shaped by those school settings. That means that all considerations of what a child can and can't do have to be broadened to include lots of other situations outside the classroom.

Most importantly, we must consider those that occur in the child's family, beyond what we can see.

That's just one reason family engagement is so critical! There's more about family engagement in chapter 5, but I hope you will keep Felina in mind as you read more about child development here and apply these ideas to the humans in your care.

**TO SPARK YOUR LEARNING...** There are many state and federal resources available to help you learn more about the foundational elements of child development. At the federal level, the U.S. Department of Health and Human Services Administration for Children and Families maintains the Head Start Early Childhood Learning and Knowledge Center (eclkc.ohs.acf.hhs.gov). They update hundreds of resources regularly with current research and best practices. Membership organizations such as the National Association for the Education of Young Children, Zero to Three, and the National Black Child Development Institute also provide resources. And your state's early childhood education division has child care resource and referral agencies, quality rating and improvement systems (QRIS), and other resources.

## Physical Development: Frameworks and Definitions

One of the main differences between early childhood education and education that students experience beyond the early years involves physical development. As children grow older, educators expect students to have critical skills necessary for learning. Students need to pay close attention to information delivered in a variety of ways. They need to keep their bodies relatively still for extended periods of time. And they need to resist distracting impulses in order to focus on the task at hand. Indeed, these expectations may exist in the classrooms into which your students will transition.

To help children develop the skills they will need, we create environments in which children can learn and practice them. In every early childhood classroom, children develop their abilities to process sensory information, to calm and control their bodies, and to maintain strong executive function skills. And while there are important cognitive aspects to each of these skills, they all are cultivated within a child's body.

A deep understanding of physical development will help you build experiences that support children's learning and growth. Once you recognize the connection between mind and body that students are establishing, you'll realize the power and joy of supporting physical development.

The part of a child's body that will produce the most remarkable development? Their brain.

## Neurological Development

Children's brains develop at astonishing rates throughout infancy and toddlerhood. The growth slows during the preschool years, but young children's brains are still rapidly developing. They are creating and modifying the building blocks for all forms of development each moment they are in your classroom. You are, truly, supporting children's neurological development for the rest of their lives. You build brains!

Different parts of the brain are responsible for different aspects of development and function. Each requires regular stimulation in order to grow. Motor regions oversee control of different parts of the body related to movement. Sensory regions oversee input from the five senses (sight, hearing, smell, taste, and touch). And association regions oversee activities that we usually refer to as "thinking." All of these regions of the brain can only grow when a child feels safe, which requires a caregiver who can provide trusted, warm, and responsive care. That's why principle 1 is first: education can only take place in a caring environment. The act of care is the foundational form of teaching.

TO SPARK YOUR LEARNING... The Harvard Center on the Developing Child provides an astounding array of articles, videos, and more related to the foundational elements of children's development. They have a special emphasis on neurological development and the impact of trauma. Learn more at developingchild.harvard.edu.

## Gross Motor Development

Any activity using a child's biggest muscles is related to *gross motor development*. Preschoolers develop their gross motor systems by using their legs, hips, backs, torsos, and arms throughout the day. They move through space, walking, running, jumping, tumbling, and skipping both indoors and outdoors. Often their energy outpaces their skills, causing them to fall over and bump into their peers.

That's because, along with muscle strength, they are developing both their balance and their sense of their bodies in space, or *proprioception*. Remember: just a few months ago, they were toddlers learning to walk. And this was happening while their centers of gravity were high in their bodies due to their massive heads! Spills and recoveries, sometimes accompanied by tears, are elemental building blocks of gross motor development.

The requirements of gross motor development demand that high-quality preschool classrooms provide many opportunities throughout the day for children to use their bodies in safe, playful activity. We now know that children require a very different environment from the "sit still and pay attention" classrooms of the past. Many children need to move their bodies throughout the day in order to pay attention. They need opportunities for gross motor activity to develop their crucial cognitive skills. Here is a suggested list of the gross motor skills your classroom activities should promote:

- climbing on safe features (ladders, rock walls) with fall areas in place that allow children to leap from safe heights

- running, stopping, restarting, falling, and getting up on their own to start running again

- throwing, catching, and kicking balls of different sizes

- walking and running up and down inclined indoor and outdoor features (stairs, berms)

- riding on toys like trikes, striding bicycles, and scooters

- walking in lines, on curves, and in circles, using small and large steps

- balancing on one or two feet on different surfaces (floors, stumps and rocks, balance beams)

## Fine Motor Development

Fine motor development involves the smaller muscles of the body, most importantly the muscles of the face and the hands. By toddlerhood, most children have learned how to grab items in a coordinated fashion. They use their vision or hearing, for example, to identify an object they want to have in their grasp, then snatch it. Preschoolers start using those muscles in coordination with their senses for far more sophisticated tasks. Most notably, they begin writing and drawing. They need lots of different kinds of practice in your classroom to develop those muscles. Most kindergarten classrooms will assume that children can manipulate writing instruments skillfully for long periods of time.

To build up those fine motor skills and the muscles they use, here is a suggested list of classroom activities:

- picking up differently sized and shaped objects in various quantities

- putting on and taking off their clothing with zippers, snaps, and buttons

- using food utensils to serve themselves and to place food in their mouths

- using art supplies (stamps, sculpture tools, finger paint, scissors)

## Perceptual and Sensory Development

During infancy and toddlerhood, children exposed to a wide array of stimuli develop their five senses in coordination. By preschool, most children have learned to coordinate sensory input with the motor skills to do what they want. For example, they can scan a classroom, locate a person they want to play with, and track that person as they walk into the block area. These are all important visual abilities children need to view the world and act within it. Similarly, what we often refer to as "paying attention" is a complex, coordinated set of tasks. It involves vision, hearing, and even one's sense of touch.

Separating the visual, auditory, and tactile signals that matter from all other input is a critical skill. For example, think of a child focusing on a teacher's voice and the book she's holding while ignoring the elbow of the child next to them and the sunlight and traffic noise streaming into the room. This skill is essential for school success and particularly for language and literacy development. As students move beyond early childhood classrooms, they will likely be expected to "pay attention" throughout the day with little support.

For this reason, you should think carefully about the sensory stimuli you introduce into your classroom. This is further discussed in chapter 3. In addition, identifying physical concerns that limit perceptual and sensory development is essential. That's why children's well-child checks with their pediatricians routinely include visual and hearing screening. Many schools, districts, and early childhood programs provide screening as well.

**TO SPARK YOUR LEARNING...** All federally funded programs and most programs that receive state funding in the United States are required to have routine hearing and vision screening for the children in their program. Identifying children who need additional supports or medical intervention early is critical to their success in preschool given the burst in language, literacy, and cognitive development that occurs at that time. (See this article for more on that: ncbi.nlm.nih.gov/pmc/articles/PMC3114988/.)

Contact your state department of education to learn what services it provides. Visit the Head Start Early Childhood Learning & Knowledge Center for hearing and vision resources (eclkc.ohs.acf.hhs.gov/physical-health/article/hearing-vision-screening).

# Special Considerations in Physical Development

## Building Persistence through Activity

When I was director of a preschool in Rhode Island and needed to have a chat with a parent at the end of the day, I would always wait with their child in the same place on the playground: the monkey bars. The bars were just under four feet high. They had two pairs of legs holding a horizontal ladder about eight feet in length. A six-inch step installed under the center enabled taller children to reach the rungs midway across. Why did I meet parents there? So that I could teach them about motor development and persistence.

Nearly every child in that program devoted hours to the monkey bars. They'd start by learning how to reach up from the step and grab a rung or climb one of the legs to do so. Then they'd learn how to grab one rung and hold it, dangling in the air. Then they'd learn to grab the next one, "walking" with their hands across the horizontal ladder, and drop off, landing on their feet. Some would progress to sitting on top of the bars themselves. The daredevils would learn how to hang upside down by their knees.

The children were demonstrating the way that stages of development progress, along with the learning traits needed to move forward. At each stage, I would scaffold their efforts, celebrating their successes and wondering aloud whether they could attack the next stage. While the parent and I chatted, we'd watch their child exert themselves. The parents often found it shocking, watching their child developing their persistence and their muscles at the same time. The child usually refused adult assistance. Gender, race, ethnicity, even height rarely mattered. Every child wanted to perform their mastery for us and then get to the next step after a celebratory pause. (We just had to make sure they were wearing pants, shorts, or skorts, not dresses or skirts!)

> Supporting children's persistence in your classroom is one of the lifelong gifts you can provide.

This cluster of developmental activities is important for all young children. Both fine and gross motor activities require gradual, constant refinement that demands activity, not complacency. And given the significant challenges this learning requires, children also develop the critical skills of resilience and persistence. They face challenges and failures while maintaining their efforts toward a goal. Meanwhile, we adults learn how to scaffold these efforts. We allow children to experience the difficulties this progress demands. And we recognize their resilience in facing challenges and their pride in demonstrating persistence.

It's important to recognize that one of the key characteristics of successful students involves persistence. While elementary classrooms can provide lots of support for children struggling with this skill, as students grow older our educational system increasingly expects them to persist on their own, with little (if any) encouragement. Supporting children's persistence in your classroom is one of the lifelong gifts you can provide.

And there's no need for special purchases or activities. Just keep your eye out for opportunities to encourage persistence. Every playground, classroom, and school has its persistence machines. Find yours and use them!

## Culture, Gender, and Motor Development

While most children in our program demonstrated interest in the monkey bars, it's important to note that motor development activities can vary greatly according to culture and gender. The expectations of families vary as well. Some families are eager for their children to participate in assertive, rough-and-tumble play, while others see such play as violent and unsafe. Your classroom could include families insistent that their children go outside every day for as much time as possible, regardless of the weather. Others may request that their children be kept inside when it is, according to them, "too hot" or "too cold." And children's sensory temperaments vary widely. Some children are alert to every possible messy activity, including ones that you'd prefer they avoid. Others are unwilling to touch anything remotely goopy or sticky.

In these situations, it's important to have a clear sense of your program's expectations. These expectations need to be consistent across rooms and teachers and explained to parents from the outset. Parent concerns about their children's development deserve respectful engagement. This will require you to explain why your motor development activities exist and what benefits they have for each child. As you do so, keep your equity lens in hand, recognizing your own biases. (Were you a rough-and-tumble child? How do you feel about chilly outdoor play?) Make sure family and child needs are always front and center.

Finally, if children resist a particular activity, it's important for you to find other activities that promote the skills related to that resisted activity. Children can tumble down a berm on their own, for example, without being bumped by other, more assertive children. In doing so, they develop their gross motor skills and proprioception just as effectively. Balancing commonality and individuality, after all, is essential for everything we do!

## Building Fine Motor Strength and Skill

Like many people, my most vivid memory of fine motor development involves the painful cramps I got as I learned how to hold a pencil to write. The transition from a barrel grip—my whole hand clenched in a fist—to a tripod grip was excruciating for me. Letter formation was far more challenging than simply trying to draw straight lines and smooth curves. Meanwhile, as a lefty, whenever I held the pencil the way all the righties did, I smudged my writing with the side of my hand. That mess required that I develop a tortured grasp that pivoted my hand over the writing, a position I use to this day. It took a long, painful time to learn. It's hard to make nice letters and draw happy stick people when your hand is throbbing!

As a result, I'm always happy to see preschool teachers encouraging a wide array of fine motor activities for children, instead of limiting them to writing and drawing. For example, consider making and using play dough; using soft and firm squishy items during play; finger painting; staging real (bread, cookies, etc.) and pretend (mud kitchen) cooking activities; and playing musical instruments. All of these experiences develop the same muscles children need to master fine motor activities for writing and drawing.

## Perception and Communication Complexity

As discussed above, "paying attention" is a complex act. And preschool classrooms are busy worlds filled with sensory stimulation. Unfortunately, you may find yourself assuming that children hear, understand, and can process the implications of a sentence you shout across a room. But even adults have a hard time hearing, understanding, and processing language in busy environments. How much more challenging is it for preschoolers developing their senses?

> Multiplying the message simply means creating opportunities for children to process information in varied ways.

For that reason, effective preschool teachers "multiply the message" in as many ways as possible when communicating. Multiplying the message simply means creating opportunities for children to process information in varied ways. In particular, multiplying the message is a reminder that saying one sentence out loud to a classroom of children is rarely a useful form of communication on its own. Instead, there are ways to multiply your message and make it more likely to be received. Cue children in advance for a message that's coming in a couple of minutes. When the time comes, state the message repeatedly, point to a visual schedule referring to the activity, and tap individual children on the shoulder to provide the message close to their ears.

Some of these efforts can become features of your classroom. For instance, you can create a daily schedule "multiplied" with numbers (times), letters (labels), and images (photos of the activity) in sequence. Refer to it regularly throughout the day with groups and individual children. Other efforts involve your moment-by-moment statements as you manage the classroom.

Let's take block center cleanup as an example. Saying "put the blocks away" is not likely to produce an organized center! Instead, consider a sequence of varied communication. Prep children a few minutes before cleanup with the basic steps. When cleanup time arrives, stand in the block area and restate the steps. Place a block on the proper location on the shelf while narrating your actions. Hand another to a nearby child while you touch their shoulder. This sequence will activate a child's vision, hearing, and touch all at once.

## Sensory Integration and Sensitivity

Multiplying the message, though a useful classroom skill for teachers, is based on the assumption that a child's senses are able to act in a coordinated manner. Researchers refer to this concept as *sensory integration*. Though this concept is still being researched, early childhood educators can benefit now from some of the insights. In particular, we know that all children benefit from environments that provide rich and varied experiences in all five senses and across all motor activity.

At the same time, a classroom can be overloaded with varied, overlapping sensory experiences. This actually prevents many children from developing the sensory integration that promotes engaged, joyful participation in classroom life. As we'll discuss more in chapter 3, it's critical to be as intentional as you can when designing your classroom environment. Provide quiet, nonsocial, and visually simple spaces and opportunities throughout the day. You may find that children with particular sensory sensitivities to noise, touch, or visual stimuli gravitate to those spaces to help them regulate.

For example, an activity involving messy goop may elicit happy giggles from most of your students. But it's possible that some students find that particular sensory input disturbing or even overwhelming. Keep an eye out for these moments of overwhelm when stimuli change. This can happen when you turn on dance party music; when you go outside into the heat, cold, or rain; and the like.

# Cognitive Development: Frameworks and Definitions

Cognitive development unfolds in dynamic relationship to other forms of development, particularly neurological. Cognition happens in the brain, which, of course, is located in the child's body. Thus it is impacted by all forms of physical development. Cognition is also impacted by children's social and emotional development, which we'll discuss later in this chapter. As our principles make clear, you can only spark learning for children who feel connected to you, the classroom environment, and their peers.

All preschool and preK curriculum and assessment approaches focus extensively on the elements of cognitive development. They identify indicators for different areas of knowledge and skill connected to literacy, numeracy, and so on. Chapter 4 discusses the best ways to approach curriculum, assessment, and instruction. Here we focus primarily on a set of particularly important topics in cognitive development for your classroom. But first, let's look at the foundational cognitive step all preschoolers need to make.

## From Preoperational Thought to Symbolic Thought

One of the great gifts preschoolers give the adults in their lives is a window into their world of thought. Cognitive development explodes in preschool, with notable milestones occurring right out in the open for everyone to see. Suddenly, children learn the first letter in their names, linking the sound to this strange shape. Or they announce that they can now count to 100 and perform the task more or less accurately. Given that most preschoolers are happy to tell you what they're thinking, you'll likely not have to ask very often to spark your learning about these exploding skills!

> Preschoolers' thinking builds from immediate sensory impressions into the world of symbolic thought, where symbols like numbers and words stand for things that cannot presently be perceived by our senses.

These recognizable skills are built on a critical shift in children's cognitive development. The work of theorist Jean Piaget helps us understand this shift. Preschoolers' thinking builds from immediate sensory impressions into the world of symbolic thought, where symbols like numbers and words stand for things that cannot presently be perceived by our senses. Symbols take up residence in our brains, aided by representations like letters and digits. Those symbols in our brains become the tools for the advanced cognitive acts like reading, writing, and arithmetic that are essential for school success.

A child recognizes that the number of blocks doesn't change whether they are stacked, arranged in a line, or piled in a heap. Another can sort small toy animals first into groups based on color and then into groups based on type of animal. A third, guided by a teacher who is reading to them, can match an item on a book's page to an item on a shelf in the room. These three children are able to activate concepts in their minds—number, category, and object definition in these examples—and use them to draw conclusions. The conclusions are different from what their senses may seem to tell them about size, similarity, and so on. These are key cognitive achievements, according to Piaget, and you will see them happening like fireworks in your classroom if you know to look for them.

## Major Concepts in Children's Cognitive Development

Conceptual thinking is not merely a cognitive skill related to toys sorted by color or shape. It unfolds throughout a class of young children in many ways. There are lots of examples of how conceptual thinking relates to your classroom community, underpinning skills that are central to school success.

The concept of time is a good example. It is a seemingly simple idea that adults often expect children to understand despite all appearances to the contrary. We've all heard preschoolers talk about how they "will see grammy yesterday," or guess that it will take at least ten minutes for that building next door to be built. Meanwhile, preschoolers live in a perpetual present. To them, anything happening right now is permanent and fixed, lasting forever—until, of course, it stops. This is especially true for events that provoke strong emotional reactions.

For young children, time is far from obvious. Rather, it's an invention that requires thoughtful approaches to teaching. We cannot assume that children already understand what we adults know.

Teaching time to preschoolers by pointing to a calendar on the wall will only confuse and overwhelm them. They can't yet comprehend and process the letters, numbers, and structure. A far better way to teach time is by multiplying the message around the routines and components of classroom life that relate to the passing of time.

For children who are developing their understanding of sequencing, the visual daily schedule provides a regular opportunity to teach "before," "now," and "later." Create a small pick-up and drop-off board with attachable photographs of children's bus drivers or family members. This allows each child to identify who brought them to school and who will be there to take them home after the school day ends. Display a three-position yesterday/today/tomorrow chart with attachable pictures of a house and a school. Use it to track how these relative concepts of time shift each day, addressing the gaps we often don't notice are there.

> Preschoolers routinely think in statements. Learning how to ask a question involves multiple cognitive steps, moving past "what I know" and into "what I don't know and want to find out."

If you're listening carefully and thinking about preschoolers' conceptual thinking, you'll see examples of these sorts of gaps all the time. Preschoolers routinely think in statements. Learning how to ask a question involves multiple cognitive steps, moving past "what I know" and into "what I don't know and want to find out." So when you're reading an informational book or exploring some new natural phenomenon on the playground, prompt for inquiry when you can and listen for the arrival of accurately constructed questions.

Finally, paying attention to children's use of conceptual categories is extremely helpful when social squabbling occurs. Children's accusations will start flying around the room, so listen carefully. Moral categories such as right and wrong, fair and unfair, and kind and hurtful seem obvious to adults. But this kind of conceptual thinking requires a similarly complex process. Designing thoughtful opportunities for children to develop their understanding of these concepts and processes takes time and a keen awareness of your preschoolers' cognitive development.

**TO SPARK YOUR LEARNING...** Learning how to provide a framework to ask provocative questions is at the heart of instruction that prompts cognitive development. In their book, *From Children's Interests to Children's Thinking: Using a Cycle of Inquiry to Plan Curriculum*, Jane Tingle Broderick and Seong Bock Hong (2020) walk through every facet of effective planning for this crucial work, from classroom design to compelling provocations to interpreting observations. In *Making and Tinkering with STEM: Solving Design Challenges with Young Children*, Cate Heroman (2017) focuses on provocations that help children delve more deeply into the cognitive foundations of science, technology, engineering, and mathematics.

# Special Considerations in Cognitive Development

## Cognitive Development Throughout Everyday Activities

Children's cognitive development is enriched through play and other everyday activities. Chatting with a baby doll while changing its diaper; asking a stuffed animal dog where it wants to go for a walk; taking the pizza order of a guest in a pretend restaurant: these types of activities happen throughout the day in a preschool classroom's pretend-play area. Each activity indicates that a child is developing a more sophisticated understanding about their imagined community members. Often without adult scaffolding, children use pretend play to build many important cognitive skills.

For this reason, as discussed in chapter 3, your classroom should have a wide variety of developmentally appropriate toys whose uses require increasing complexity and more challenging problem-solving. Simply learning what a toy is for, what sorts of play it can and can't provide, is a problem-solving opportunity. Can I stack these curved blocks on top of each other? What happens if I knock them down? Do the wheels on this truck allow me to push it fast and in both directions? Or is it different from the truck I used yesterday? What do those colored bubbles do if I turn the bottle upside down, and why? Object characteristics, causality, problem-solving, memory, questioning—all of these cognitive skills are developed in these "simple" play experiences.

Similarly, foundational math concepts and skills can be activated throughout your classroom. Numbers, quantity, and spatial relationships can often be taught in playful ways. Shapes and geometric features are part of children's lives and readily available throughout your classroom. Cylindrical cups, rectangular paper, and concave cubbies provide great opportunities to name and discuss the features of each. Meanwhile, nearly everything in the classroom can be characterized, sorted, ordered, and/or counted. Often these concepts need only to be pointed out by a teacher. For example, you can indicate which objects go above and which go below when putting toys back on the shelf. Or you can sequence classroom cleanup tasks into first, next, and last in preparation to go outside.

> Simply learning what a toy is for, what sorts of play it can and can't provide, is a problem-solving opportunity.

In this way, everyday activities, play, classroom maintenance, and more can be activated for learning complex concepts that advance cognitive development. There's a place for direct instruction and precisely defined activities that teach academic concepts, which is covered in chapter 4. But a well-designed classroom provides dozens of opportunities by itself. You only need to notice and scaffold them.

## Teaching Problem-Solving

A child drops a toy and it breaks. A fun outdoor activity is put on hold due to a thunderstorm. A child rips the page of a beloved book in the library area. All of these instances are emergent opportunities for adults to scaffold individual and collective problem-solving. The learning is more likely to stick with children when it's tied to an emotional event.

The first step of effective problem-solving with children is simply a question of the adult's attitude. When a problem arises, you have two simple options. You can demonstrate an unproductive way of approaching the situation—complaining, sighing, and blaming someone else. Or you can recognize that this problem has presented a rich teaching moment, and declare to all exactly what has happened and what the problem is. Simply doing this sets the tone for a lively instructional opportunity.

Next, in collaboration with your students and any other adults in the room, you can set the stage for effective problem-solving. Start by determining the situation: What happened? Has it happened before? Why did it happen? These questions all reference history and causality. You are gathering the information that will allow for more effective problem-solving. And remember that "why" is a question about contributing factors. It's not an invitation to place blame, which is something you may need to remind preschoolers—and yourself!

Next, collect options from the community to address the problem. What can adults do? What can children do? And are there things that can be done to prevent this from happening ever again? When you've gathered your options, it's time to determine a plan and execute it step-by-step. Involve children in as much of the activity as possible, and describe each step as you go.

Finally, once you've executed the agreed-upon plan, evaluate the outcome. Did the group choose the right solution to the problem? Were there other solutions that could have worked better? And don't forget to use principle 7 to celebrate your successes and rethink any flops.

## From Egocentrism to a Theory of Mind

There is a critical cognitive component to social life that deserves mention here. Preschool classrooms are extremely complex social environments filled with young humans who are just getting to know themselves as social beings. Being surrounded by a room full of other children at this same developmental stage makes each child's social development very challenging indeed. And there's an additional impediment to that development for younger preschoolers: their egocentrism—their utterly typical, if routinely exasperating, narcissistic focus on themselves at every moment.

This egocentrism is a healthy, critical part of child development, one that may frustrate adults tired of hearing "Mine!" throughout the day. So it's especially important to recognize how a healthy self-concept is the basis for a child's necessary assertiveness, self-care, and autonomy. It's also the foundation for understanding that others have a lot more in common with them than they can fully see at first.

This is tied to a critical conceptual development that researchers call *theory of mind*. This means recognizing that other people have thoughts, feelings, and perceptions—that their minds are just like my own. For example, an egocentric child grabs a cookie from another child who immediately erupts in a distraught tantrum. The child who took the cookie might stand still with astonishment while watching the drama unfold. They are completely unable to comprehend what they just caused to happen. Their mind might think something along the lines of, "I saw that cookie and wanted it. I took it for myself. What's happening over there?" But a child who is developing a theory of mind about other children would begin to see it differently. They see that their wanting, acting, and getting that cookie had a related parallel in the mind of the sobbing child: "He wanted that cookie like I did. So he is unhappy that I took it."

> Preschool classrooms are extremely complex social environments filled with young humans who are just getting to know themselves as social beings.

When a child develops a theory of mind, they can understand that others have thoughts and feelings like their own. This powerful cognitive insight affects nearly every aspect of social life. It is the foundation of critical values like compassion and empathy. Before a child can recognize another human's rights, they need to possess the concept that there exist other humans like them who think, feel, desire, and so on—that is, indeed, what makes them human in the first place.

The implications of this one concept for early childhood professionals are vast. Recognizing others is a developmental skill, not an inbred moral law. So if you find yourself labeling children as "selfish," "mean," or "bad," consider principle 10. It's time to see things from that child's perspective. They're not a "spoiled brat"; rather, they have not yet developed this crucial concept—and they need your assistance in doing so. You can support children's development of a theory of mind. Help children observe characters in books and people in real life as they negotiate the world, react positively and negatively, and make choices. Draw parallels to children's own thinking and actions.

# Language and Literacy Development: Frameworks and Definitions

For many preschool teachers, the most exciting aspect of our job is watching as children explode into language and early literacy. A child who entered the classroom reluctant to say more than "yes" or "no" starts stringing together sentences nonstop to anyone who will listen. Someone who struggled to learn the first letter of their name works hard for many weeks—and then suddenly it just clicks. They can spell the whole thing! It's a period of growth that is rapid, easy to perceive, and repeatedly worthy of celebration.

We celebrate because language and literacy development is truly hard work! The understanding that a world of symbols surrounds all of us is a thrilling yet daunting realization. Figuring out how little straight lines and curves become letters and words and sentences takes lots of sustained effort, persistence, and resilience. Confronting the limits of one's oral language while building one's vocabulary is a daily challenge. This is always most apparent when a child really wants something and can't express it. The hard work to build language and literacy skills is happening all the time in your preschool classroom, and the rewards are quite literally endless.

## Five Areas of Language Development

As children develop their language skills, whether mono- or multilingually, they do so in five distinct but related areas. (Some lists include a sixth area, *orthography*, which refers to written symbols such as letters, numerals, signs, and the like.) While these five areas of development often unfold in sequence, we want to always recognize that no two children develop language skills in the same way or order. Everyone typically jumps between the areas depending on different situations, levels of fluency, content areas, and so on.

## Phonology

Preschoolers are already familiar with the sounds that they can produce orally. This is thanks to their use of sounds when developing productive nonverbal communication as infants. *Phonology* refers to developing an understanding of the way that sounds are organized and used. Each language has its own set of speech sounds. Those sounds involve many subtleties related to pronunciation, intonation, and the ability to make the sound with the voice box, tongue, and mouth.

Let's take my attempts to learn Spanish as an example. I have been able to learn most of the basic phonology: *ll* does not make an /el/ sound but is pronounced like the letter *y* in English; the letter *ñ* does not make the same sound as the letter *n*. But while my phonology is pretty sound in theory, in practice I still have gaps. I still can't roll my *r*'s, for example, despite years of trying.

These subtleties of sound show up in our accents, where two people might pronounce the exact same word in wildly different ways, and also in the meaning of what we say. For example, when someone "uptalks," raising the pitch of their voice at the end of a statement, the intonation shift suggests a question instead of a statement. As preschoolers develop their language fluency, they are confronted with all these subtle phonological challenges.

## Morphology

Preschoolers encounter another set of subtle challenges that relate to *morphology*, the study of all things related to the form and structure of words. Morphology includes the rules we use for making certain words with parts called *morphemes*, such as adding the suffix −*ed* to a root verb to indicate the past tense (paint + −ed = painted, for example). Understanding when such suffixes are appropriate and when they are not is an important skill for preschoolers. It takes some effort to understand and remember that "I painted yesterday" is correct but "I drawed yesterday" is wrong!

Morphology also concerns the rules we use to categorize words in various ways, not only by tense, but by case, number, and so on. Preschoolers will often demonstrate their understanding of these rules by making errors related to them. For example, a child who says, "Look at the turtles and fishes in the tank!" is using the rule of adding −*s* to indicate more than one of a category. They are demonstrating a successful use of language. When you point out that "fish" is, strangely enough, both singular and plural in number, you should celebrate the correct use of −*s* as well. Approaching "mistakes" like "drawed" and "fishes" as signs of linguistic development is a key part of language instruction in every early childhood classroom.

## Semantics

As every preschooler will be happy to demonstrate, they are also learning about semantics. *Semantics* is the relationship between words and their meanings. Children's enthusiasm is understandable, because this is a fascinating cognitive project. After weeks of learning the meaning of one word, such as *ball*, they suddenly realize that this word-and-meaning combination applies to everything in their world. They start assigning names and labels to things. Their brains become sponges for this expansion of their oral vocabulary. Indeed, preschoolers are remarkably skilled at learning new words and being able to use them almost immediately.

Part of the cognitive project involves learning the boundaries of various words and their meanings. Many babies learn that their pet is a *dog*, to the delight of their caregivers, who are then amused when, on a trip to the zoo, each elephant, giraffe, and tiger is also a *dog*. The converse of this overgeneralization is overrestriction, when a child insists that their *house* is the one and only house on the street. After all, that's the only one they've been in! Helping children contract and expand the meanings of words takes some skill. But with practice it can become one of the truly enjoyable challenges of your work as a preschool teacher.

Another important component of semantics involves the different vocabularies and meanings children may hear in the different settings in which they spend their time. Like accents, the use and meanings of specific words can be quite different in the classroom, at home, or at grandma's house. This is particularly the case for children who are learning two or more languages at once. In its early stages, this often results in one vocabulary with many words taken from each language.

A successful preschool teacher will help children negotiate those differences without prioritizing one approach to language as the "right" way of speaking. A bilingual teacher is a wonderful gift to bilingual preschool children for this and many other reasons. Indeed, negotiating and switching between various forms of language is an important skill for all children. They need that understanding and fluency to use language in its most powerful forms.

## Syntax

As children develop a set of words and meanings into their working vocabulary, they begin to assemble those words to communicate effectively. The arrangement of words into sentences is referred to as *syntax*. Most children start with brief two- or three-word sentences made only of active verbs or nouns. Later they add linking verbs or prepositions. As they develop their syntactic skills, children start building longer sentences. These sentences often don't follow some of the basic rules for word order, independent clause length, and so on.

Syntax can be very different from one language to the next. This needs to be considered if a child is learning more than one language. For example, in English syntax, adjectives go in front of nouns. In many other languages, adjectives follow nouns, a significant syntactic difference. Similarly, different languages treat verb tenses in various ways. In English, the addition of short morphemes like *—ed* and

—*ing* at the end of words is also a syntactic skill. Prepositional phrases, independent and dependent clauses, even questions: all of these language elements fall under the umbrella of syntax.

## Pragmatics

On top of phonology, morphology, semantics, and syntax, preschoolers have one additional element of language to master. For some children it's the most complex of all. Language is a tool of communication comprised of different elements. Learning how to assemble those different elements appropriately in different situations is called *pragmatics*. Here are a few examples of the skillful use of pragmatics: communicating your need or desire, participating in a particular social group as an active member, and persuading someone to do one thing and not another.

As you probably have guessed, any discussion of pragmatics requires us to lean into principle 4 and get out our equity lens. Many of the features of "appropriate" language use are culturally determined. While they may feel "normal" to us, they are not an inherent part of a language. Instead, those features of language relate to the ways that a particular language is used by particular people in particular situations. The social, cultural, and regional aspects of language use all fall under the category of pragmatics.

Let's take a look at some of the social rules of language that might at first glance appear to be value neutral. We find, upon inspection, that they reveal a very particular cultural bias. In many classrooms, children are expected to take turns talking and not interrupt each other; one speaker follows another speaker in sequential monologues. This may appear to be a "polite" way to conduct circle time. However, it is in fact a particular feature of language use in many Euro-American communities, one that is not shared elsewhere. In other communities, individuals are happy to talk while others are talking. They process information collectively, in a manner that some teachers might consider rude. But this use of language is not a form of interruption. Rather, it's a different approach to language pragmatics, one where collective language processing is privileged over individual sequential speaking.

Identifying differences in pragmatics in your classroom is very important! The challenge is in avoiding the judgments that often follow from our recognition of those differences. Several years ago, I was doing a presentation to several dozen senior citizens volunteering in schools. The monolingual English speakers sat silently in the front rows. They made eye contact with me and listened intently to my presentation, nodding politely. Meanwhile, a group of Spanish-speaking seniors sat in the back, discussing the various points I was making, often with great enthusiasm. At the end, one of the volunteers sitting in the front row approached me to complain about the "rude behavior" in the back of the room. I responded that, as far as I could tell, those folks were the most engaged participants I had ever had at a training!

Being "polite," not talking too much or being too quiet, making or failing to make eye contact, adjusting your volume up or down—all of these are elements of pragmatics that you may have strong opinions about. Our speech is deeply connected to our sense of identity, which is deeply connected to our sense of values and appropriate behavior. So as a preschool teacher you need to be extra careful to keep your equity lens focused on your own pragmatics biases. This is especially important when you hear judgment creeping in about the way a child or a family member is choosing to express themselves.

## From Language to Literacy

Some preschoolers seem to enter the world of print—letters, written words, reading, and writing—easily and rapidly, in bursts that surprise adults. Other preschoolers appear to enter literacy more slowly. They transition from speech and language into the symbolic world of letters at a pace that can alarm teachers and family members both.

> Unlike speech, which infants begin to develop as soon as they are born, our brains do not naturally build the capacity for written language. That means every child needs explicit instruction in order to learn about letters, written words, and reading.

These differences should not be surprising, and the recent conversations on the science of reading help us understand why they exist. As long as humans have walked the earth, our brains have been wired to speak what we hear. Learning speech is a natural feature of all human existence. Across cultures and languages, speech is an artifact of hundreds of thousands of years of human brain development.

But our brains are not wired to read. Writing is a relatively recent phenomenon in human society. It is a technology that's only a few thousand years old, and our brains have not yet caught up to that recent technological development. Unlike speech, which infants begin to develop as soon as they are born, our brains do not naturally build the capacity for written language. That means every child needs explicit instruction in order to learn about letters, written words, and reading. Every preschool teacher needs to know the basics of supporting children's transition from auditory language to print.

These instructional basics do not include drill-and-kill activities or worksheets. Those and other similar methods set aside our commitment to developmentally appropriate practice and play-based learning! Rather, as we shift our focus from general language development to literacy, it is important to provide varied literacy experiences, emphasizing a play-based, engaging approach with many options. We also want to include responsive additions for children who, for whatever reason, are resistant to or not benefitting from those activities. Here are some core elements of preschool literacy development.

## Preschool Writing

As children develop their symbolic understanding—recognizing that something can stand in for something else—they begin to recognize the importance of drawing and writing. Using a marker, crayon, or pencil, a child can create something that is symbolic of something else and that carries meaning for others. That realization is the foundation for all aspects of writing.

Many sequences have been created to track the development of emergent writing skills. In the NAEYC journal *Young Children*, Teresa A. Byington and YaeBin Kim (2017) detail nine stages as follows.

1. Drawings that represent writing.

2. Scribbling, a form of mark-making that the child intends to be writing that carries meaning.

3. Wavy scribbles or mock writing from left to right.

4. Marks in letter-like shapes.

5. Recognizable letters assembled in strings but not as words.

6. Transitional writing forms: copied words found in the environment, such as books, labels, or posters, or letters assembled in groups with spaces between them.

7. Invented or phonetic spelling, in which the letters chosen represent the sounds found in actual words. Often the first and last letter represent the sounds found at the start and end of the word (for example, *DG* for *dog*).

8. Beginning word and phrase writing, with letter sounds in the middle of words added and short phrases appearing.

9. Conventional spelling and sentence writing.

At each of these stages of writing development, small insights lead to major steps forward in skill development. The transition from scribbling to letter-like marks shows a child's appreciation for the discrete elements of print we call letters. You can scaffold that child's insight by helping them recognize these discrete elements in a variety of print examples in your classroom. A child who is ready to start using invented or phonetic spelling is at a later stage of conceptual understanding. This child is ready to discuss the sounds that particular letters represent, often starting with the first letter of their name.

Each of these stages of writing is linked to a major cognitive step forward in the understanding of print. A skillful preschool teacher understands the conceptual foundation they can use to scaffold a child's development, building the next foundational element of these emergent writing skills. Using the print-rich environment you've created (discussed in chapter 3), you have many opportunities to help a child engage that concept in more contexts, using signs, book covers, cubby labels, and even junk mail to help reinforce these crucial foundations. In this way, knowing that using writing utensils requires ever-more-skilled fine motor control, you can help a child develop their writing away from the writing desk or table.

## Preschool Reading Development

As the discussion of writing made clear, the entry into print has many component parts, all of which are necessary for children to develop into proficient readers. But the science of reading shows us that the process requires even more substantial skills and knowledge. Children need to understand the wide array of sounds that letters and words use, particularly in the apparent jumble of the English language. (For example, try explaining the *—ough* sounds in *through, cough, dough,* and *bough* to a preschooler!) Children need to develop the content frames—or schemas—featured in books in order to make meaning of the words. They need to recognize what happens in a forest, on a farm, or at a grocery store. And children need a huge vocabulary that allows them to draw meaning from most of the words on the page.

Following the guidance of the science of reading, we can think of reading as having five key components for preschool classrooms.

**Phonological and Phonemic Awareness.** Phonological awareness refers to the ability to recognize and manipulate the sounds of spoken language. A critical subset of this involves phonemic awareness, the understanding that words are made of individual sounds called *phonemes*. Awareness of these sounds can be taught in ways that support children's reading development. You can promote phonological awareness with activities such as rhyming games and alliterative songs, encouraging children to listen to and identify these distinct sounds that help build their foundation for reading.

**Phonics.** Phonemic awareness is essential to understanding phonics, the key bridge between speech and writing. Phonics connects awareness of sounds (phonemes) to the written letters (or *graphemes*) that are associated with those sounds. Preschoolers need to recognize that letters represent specific sounds in words. Using letters that are important to individual children (such as the first letter in their first name, often the first letter/sound combination a child learns) in playful, emergent ways is effective for building this awareness. Throughout the day, you have dozens of opportunities to make the connection between letters and sounds both explicit and fun.

**Vocabulary.** Developing a useful collection of words that help us explain and learn about the world is another key skill. Though children will build their reading and writing vocabulary largely after preschool, your classroom is a wonderful environment in which to build their listening and speaking vocabulary. These vocabularies expand when you expose preschoolers to a rich and diverse range of words in your interactions. Reading aloud is critical, to be sure. Other effective strategies include sharing and discussing stories, exploring new words in context, and expanding from simple words to more nuanced ones.

> Though children will build their reading and writing vocabulary largely after preschool, your classroom is a wonderful environment in which to build their listening and speaking vocabulary.

**Comprehension.** Vocabulary can be a vehicle to develop early comprehension skills. These skills include accumulating the background knowledge within which new vocabulary emerges. They also include learning new comprehension strategies, like asking questions about stories, predicting what might happen next, and making connections between stories and one's own experiences. These skills involve thinking about thinking: What do I want to know about? What do I think will happen next? How does this story refer to things in my life? Thinking about thinking is known as *metacognition*, a foundation of all critical thinking. You can foster this critical skill in your classroom with thoughtful, responsive questions to individual children and groups.

**Print Concepts.** As they add to their understanding of speech, children need to develop understanding of the rules and features of print in this strange new world of language. Quality preschool classrooms are print-rich environments—but they avoid meaningless wall clutter that children can't see and teachers never use. Examples of good materials to use are cubby labels, room schedules, meal menus, and book titles. Environmental print gives you opportunities to teach print concepts like text direction (left to right), the distinction between letters and words and the spacing between them, and the roles of punctuation and letter case.

There are other elements to reading, such as *fluency*, the ability to read with accuracy and speed, that develop in later stages. The science of reading warns us not to push past playful, engaging exploration of language and literacy into these later stages. They are more typically developed when children have the foundational skills listed above. We'll talk in chapters 3, 4, and 5 about how to create the environments and instruction to build these skills. And we'll talk about collaborative ways to engage families to do the same.

TO SPARK YOUR LEARNING... There are tremendous resources helping our field integrate all that we know about the science of reading. Jodene L. Smith's *What the Science of Reading Says: Literacy Strategies for Early Childhood* (2023) does a great job of exploring how you can bring these powerful insights into your classroom.

# Special Considerations in Language and Literacy Development

## Babies and Productive Preverbal Communication

To fully understand preschooler language development, it's best to start with the earliest days of infancy. Shortly after birth, most infants become aware that their needs will be met if they can communicate them to their adult caregivers. Babies are ingenious about sophisticated preverbal communication! One easy way to perceive this is to go to a grocery store where infants and toddlers roam the aisles with their caregivers. Just a few minutes of observation will reveal to you that each child has determined ways to communicate their desires to a particular adult, sometimes to humorous effect.

However humorous they may look and sound, those forms of asking, pleading, whining, and demanding are the result of weeks and months of hard work on the part of that child. Each baby has learned the forms of communication that work best with those particular adult caregivers. Those babbles, whines, and screams might not work on you, a stranger, when you're trying to grab a box of cereal. But they happen because they work on the adults who matter to that child!

Before they become adept at oral language, babies develop a set of productive communication skills. Babies learn about the power of tone, volume, and sound. They learn this even before they develop the understanding that those components can be arranged systematically into words. That awareness of the components of language stays with children throughout preschool—it's why telling a whining child to "use your regular voice" often works! You will be a more effective teacher if you recognize the subtle forms of communication that develop in infancy and require greater adult attention.

Looking at an object for a sustained period of time; turning their head toward a sound; reaching a hand out toward a person walking across the room: all of these are nonverbal forms of productive communication. They are critical behaviors for infants and preverbal toddlers. These forms of communication remain important as children develop their oral language proficiency in your preschool classroom. In particular, these cues are critical for children struggling with language development or developing their understanding of a second language. Keep an eye out for them.

## The Importance of Storytelling

As preschoolers move from speech into the world of reading and writing, early childhood educators need to recognize that the critical importance of oral language hasn't diminished. And stories matter a great deal! Storytelling components such as placing experiences in order, processing them as oral narrative, and engaging others in the experience play vital roles in many of the world's families and cultures. They also provide opportunities to develop many of the foundational skills for language and literacy listed above.

Storytelling is a form of making meaning, not just a mechanism for creative invention. The knowledge bases of many religions and cultures rely on storytelling as the repository of ancestral histories and spiritual insights. Many families are built around history that is shared from one generation to another. Creating opportunities to listen to and share stories, however simple or complex, can be a part of any preschool classroom. These moments can be impromptu—activities that unfold when other, less engaging tasks are happening. For example, waiting in line to go outside can be an opportunity to talk about what happened over the weekend. And children are always happy to talk at the lunch table about their morning and evening routines for personal grooming, food consumption, and much more.

Finally, infant mental health professionals tell us that children who have experienced difficult situations often reach out to trusted adults to share those experiences. Being a trustworthy adult involves anticipating new or challenging situations unfolding in a child's life, such as a home move, the arrival of a new family member, or an extended illness. Learn about how to scaffold this storytelling in chapter 5.

# Social and Emotional Development: Frameworks and Definitions

In many ways, children's social and emotional development is the beating heart of quality early childhood environments. When education and care are linked (principle 1), children develop a sense of belonging connected to their whole self, on both good days and bad. When you help children celebrate successes and reflect on challenges (principle 7), the classroom becomes a supportive environment. In this type of classroom, you can work on whatever aspects of social and emotional development are most alive at that moment.

Most importantly, children's abilities to regulate their emotions and their resulting behaviors has a huge impact on their social inclusion and on their foundational experience of schooling. Your classroom has the power to support children as they work on these skills. This helps establish and build children's confidence that school can be a place of successful achievement for years to come.

## Recognizing Clusters of Attachment Behaviors

Attachment is a critical component of every quality early childhood classroom. But the way that the ECE field thinks about attachment has shifted significantly in recent years. Those shifts mean that we now view attachment not as one thing, but as a set of possible responsive opportunities for connection. These are not optional: as our first principle states, education is care and care is education. Every successful preschool classroom operates on responsive, attached relationships.

> Our job is to observe children carefully and determine what creates a secure, trustworthy relationship with an adult. We need to be flexible in our approach to each child.

For decades, attachment was understood to relate to a specific set of adult behaviors to which all children respond. We now understand that perspective to be a culturally specific definition. It doesn't apply to many other communities across the globe, including those represented by families in your classroom. Instead, as early childhood professionals, we seek to understand what each child needs from adults to create and maintain secure attachments.

That can be tricky indeed! Consider touch. We know that caregiver touch is incredibly important for infants, especially for newborns. But by the time an older child gets to your classroom, other factors and experiences may have affected that child's relationship to touch. Some children seek out extremely strong, high-pressure contact with others. Other children avoid being touched as much as possible. Some children's responses are deeply situational: they want to be hugged when they are distraught and left completely alone as soon as they stop crying.

Our job is to observe children carefully and determine what creates a secure, trustworthy relationship with an adult. We need to be flexible in our approach to each child. A child who resists touch may appreciate you sitting near them, commenting on what they're doing but not giving them an unwanted hug. Of course, if you desperately want to hug that child, your impulse is saying something important about your own attachment biases!

**TO SPARK YOUR LEARNING...** *Babies*, the 2010 French documentary film by Thomas Balmès, provides an outstanding opportunity to consider parenting and attachment in the first year across four different cultures. The babies featured in the film are Bayarjargal (Bayar) from Bayanchandmani, Mongolia; Hattie from San Francisco; Mari from Tokyo, Japan; and Ponijao from Opuwo, Namibia. Throughout the film, you watch the children in many different settings. They are in rural and urban locations, alone and with others, playing and crying and eating—and there is no voiceover "explaining" what you're seeing. The variations among the four situations are remarkable. You may find that some differences make you ponder your own reactions! That is, in large part, the point of the film: the lack of narration leaves you to interpret it on your own. This could be a great movie night option for you and your colleagues. Together you can watch four children develop into healthy preschoolers, and you can talk openly about what you do and don't think parenting and attachment should be. This can help your team learn their own preferences, values, and biases.

## Stages of Play

Nearly a century ago, researcher Mildred Parten determined that there are five stages of play that you are likely to see in your preschool classroom. It is true that children ultimately need to learn how to collaborate; however these five stages do not necessarily describe a progression. Rather, they describe the different forms of play that children are likely to take part in with different peers, in different situations, and on different days.

- When a child is sitting alone and showing little interest in the things or people around them, they are in the first stage, *unoccupied behavior*. As always, it's important to resist the urge to jump to conclusions about what this behavior means. It could mean that the child is spending some quiet alone time after a period of intense activity. It could mean that the child has attempted to enter play but was unable to do so. These are but two of many possible unoccupied situations, and they require very different responses from a teacher.

- The next stage is similar but refers to a child who seems to be more attentive to what's happening around them: *onlooker behavior*. In these situations, the child is observing what's going on and seems to be interested in it. But they aren't interacting with things or people: they are just watching intently. Like with unoccupied behavior, you'll want to be sensitive to the different meanings of onlooker behavior.

- The third stage is *parallel play*. Like parallel lines, children engaging in parallel play are side by side, doing similar things, but not touching at all. There's no interaction between the children directly. You can infer that the children are aware of each other due to the similarities in their activity. For example, if two children are blowing bubbles with straws outside or rocking baby dolls in dramatic play without directly interacting with each other, they are in parallel play.

- The fourth stage is *associative play*, in which children are playing on their own but interacting with each other. They may be talking together, perhaps sharing materials, all while pursuing their own projects. Associative play happens often in the block area, where one child is building a castle and another child is building a highway—two separate projects in which the builders may chat and even pass blocks from one to another.

- If those children decide to link the highway and the castle to build a village, they are in the fifth and final stage—*cooperative play*. Unlike associative play, where children pursue their own projects, in cooperative play children share one theme. They work collaboratively to make plans, take on different roles, and problem-solve.

Identifying these stages of play is very helpful in a preschool classroom. You can use your skills of observation to support children learning how to enter into these social situations. If a child is acting as an onlooker, it might be that they are trying to determine what other children are doing. You can assist them by describing what's happening. What are the children doing? What roles are they playing? What are the rules connected to that? Are they sharing materials? Are they taking turns? Do some children have to wait while others act?

The social process unfolding in front of the onlooker is complex. Your verbal description of the hard-to-see components of play as they occur can scaffold children's participation. To be sure, sometimes children choose not to play because they don't want to. But often, the complexities of preschool social interactions are so overwhelming that a child simply doesn't know what to do. This complexity is increased if the child has not yet developed a theory of mind, is new to the classroom, or does not speak the language other children are using.

> Teaching both skillful observation of and entry into play is an important and powerful form of instruction in every preschool classroom. It is a foundation of social-development scaffolding.

Observing stages of play requires that you activate principle 10 and work to see things from a child's perspective. Though obvious to us, children's actions can seem random to each other, without any clear cause. You can help a child identify those causes by stating the unspoken rules, interpersonal expectations, and other features of play that would be obvious to an adult. Teaching both skillful observation of and entry into play is an important and powerful form of instruction in every preschool classroom. It is a foundation of social-development scaffolding.

## Adult Social Referencing

Of course, one of the important elements of teaching children entry into play is entering into play yourself! Participating actively in children's play is one of the hallmarks of a quality early childhood classroom. Recent research has confirmed that children learn a tremendous amount from the adults around them. They learn not only about social behavior, but also about emotions, their regulation, and their expression.

Babies start picking up these insights early in life through a process called *social referencing*. This process helps them understand what they should do and feel in different situations by referring to the adult caregivers in their world. The process continues throughout early childhood and well beyond. Taking advantage of your role in social referencing is one of your magic wands in a preschool classroom.

One particularly powerful opportunity takes quite a bit of practice and collaboration with the adults in your room, but it's worth it! Reread the section on page 30, "Teaching Problem-Solving." Now, instead of a problem created by a child, let's imagine a problem created by an adult: a co-teacher forgets to set up for lunch, or steps out of the room for a personal call, leaving you alone. These sorts of problems happen all the time, as we know! But usually they go unaddressed, leaving frustration

> Recent research has confirmed that children learn a tremendous amount from the adults around them. They learn not only about social behavior, but also about emotions, their regulation, and their expression.

and annoyance lingering in the air like a fog—a fog that every person, young and old, can sense.

Let's face it: preschool classrooms are problem-generating machines for both the children in the room and the adults. And, just like problems children create, adult-generated problems provide opportunities to demonstrate thoughtful approaches to problem-solving and emotional regulation!

First, you need to check your brain state and make sure that you're responding thoughtfully, not merely reacting. This may be hard to do if your colleague has made the same error for the umpteenth time and it's driving you crazy! So why not start practicing adjusting your attitude when *you* create a problem for the classroom?

You start the process exactly as before. Recognize that your snafu presents a great opportunity to teach something important. Adjust your attitude, say what you just did, and admit the emotion that goes with it. "Oh my goodness, I dropped that pitcher of milk on the floor! How frustrating!" It seems silly, but stating what happened typically erases any tension in the room. Suddenly, everyone realizes that, after all, it's just spilled milk. The rest of the process is exactly the same as with child-created problems. Collaborate to determine what happened and why. Gather options, execute your plan together, and evaluate the outcome.

Throughout the process, cut yourself some slack. As principle 6 reminds us, you have to do the best with what you've got. Sad though it may be, you are, permanently, a fallible human being who makes mistakes, just like the rest of us. But it's not sad for a struggling child to observe your failings. If they are frustrated trying to figure out a complicated social interaction or how to spell their name, your failings are a relief! That's because you are sharing an important human truth: we are all, adults and children both, always working on something.

## Balancing Autonomy and Community Belonging

To support children's social and emotional development, a high-quality preschool classroom is always trying to balance individuality and commonality. These insights from NAEYC's position statement on developmentally appropriate practice apply not only to child development frameworks but also to the classroom context itself.

As preschool children develop socially and emotionally, they pivot between two seemingly different behaviors that are actually intertwined—socially interactive behaviors and independent behaviors. Social development means that preschoolers routinely behave in assertively independent ways. As an early childhood educator, you need to recognize that what may first seem like defiance is likely an effort at fierce autonomy. It is not a relentless form of noncompliance designed to push your last button. (Not always easy to recognize!)

But independence does not mean isolation. Preschool classrooms must treat a child's autonomy as a feature of the community itself. This autonomy is a necessary condition of belonging; a community that includes them does so by recognizing their autonomous, individual personhood.

Autonomy and community go hand in hand. Therefore, every preschool classroom needs to give each child clear entry points into belonging. These entry points are not merely community agreements or rules with which children must comply. Rather, you need to create regular, routine opportunities for children to be heard, recognized, and respected as human beings. A warm, positive classroom scaffolds children's social and emotional development. Rituals can include welcoming children and their families each day, recognizing children who are absent, celebrating efforts and successes for each child, and responding attentively to challenging situations and emotions as they arise.

> Rituals can include welcoming children and their families each day, recognizing children who are absent, celebrating efforts and successes for each child, and responding attentively to challenging situations and emotions as they arise.

This attention to belonging becomes particularly powerful as children grow older and more sophisticated in their understanding of group norms, inclusion, and exclusion. I've walked into hundreds of preschool classrooms in my life. Within a few minutes I can recognize children with strong social skills coalescing in an energetic cluster. Others are off to the side observing that popular group without access to it, and a few are either actively rejected or largely neglected.

And, often, I observe that the children who have advanced social skills and thus need less guidance from teachers are precisely the ones to whom teachers devote the most attention. Meanwhile, some of the children who need adult support the most buzz around the room disruptively, generating negative reactions from teachers. Other quiet children avoid the fray and drift alone unnoticed.

Peer status within the collective social development of a classroom community is an important element to recognize and address precisely for these reasons. Early childhood education is founded on an ethic of care that insists that we do the best we can for each child according to their needs. Every child deserves support to help them prepare for elementary school ahead. And children who have developed behaviors that either disrupt a classroom or allow them to float unnoticed within it are most vulnerable.

I believe that we have a moral obligation to serve these rejected and neglected children. When they leave our care, it is sadly unlikely that they will encounter adults with the time and training to support these complex social and emotional needs.

# Special Considerations in Social and Emotional Development

## Behaviors That Are Challenging

Without question, the topic that comes up most often in my discussions with early childhood faculty involves what some teachers call "challenging behavior." So let's devote this entire special considerations section to that topic.

Let's start by referring to the topic as "behaviors that are challenging" instead of "challenging behaviors." This reflects a slight but important change in the wording. This new wording raises an essential question: Challenging for whom? Everyone? A few people? Your family? Your community? Just you?

Whenever we start talking about behaviors that are challenging, other words start getting complicated as well. For example, I routinely hear adults say that children don't "listen." Usually, that word refers to an activity a child does with their ears. But in many classrooms, the word refers to something a child does with the rest of their body. The assumption is that a child who "listens" will automatically comply. That means that what they should be listening to is a statement directing them to do something—an instruction or order. The outcome of "listening" should be to do that instruction or order.

To make matters even more complicated, children who aren't "listening" in this way often get very confusing information from us! They need clear, developmentally appropriate instructions and steps they can follow and perform. Instead, adults often tell children what not to do in the moment that they are doing that thing! In these instances, what children need from adults is to know expectations before and after that challenging moment instead of during it.

These adult behaviors belie a fundamental misunderstanding about child development. Most early childhood educators have no problem teaching behaviors related to using eating utensils, putting together a puzzle, or holding a pencil. I've watched teachers devote hours to supporting a child's tripod grip as they master their letter writing. But there is another set of largely social behaviors that often go unnamed or untaught. And it is those very behaviors that adults assume children refuse to do. Yet those children usually haven't had opportunities to learn them in the first place.

## Teaching Behavior Expectations

Whenever I facilitate a training on child behavior development for teachers or parents, I always ask the participants to raise their hands if they teach children how to wait. Routinely, nearly everyone in the room raises their hands. After all, who hasn't told their children to wait?

But then I clarify my question by providing a deeper, and very familiar, explanation of what I mean by "teaching" children how to wait. I demonstrate the familiar instructional strategies we use in early childhood, such as verbal explanations, role modeling, and real-world opportunities to learn. Then I mention eating with utensils, completing puzzles, and writing with a pencil. I stress that, just as with those skills, we should accept repeated failure, emphasize effort, and provide dozens of opportunities for a child to learn a behavior before we expect them to know how to do it. Finally, having reviewed these basic elements of early childhood education (covered in chapter 4), I ask the question again. I rarely see more than one or two lonely hands in the air.

It's hard to name this set of untaught behaviors, but you probably can recognize a few in addition to waiting. Do we really teach children to take turns? Or do we expect them to know how to identify and resist their urges while standing patiently in line behind other children? And what about those lines? Do we really teach what a line is in concrete, specific ways, indicating exactly how close to another child is too close? Do we teach how far away means you're "not in line"? And what are we asking children to do when we tell them to "listen"?

As you can see, there's a lot to unpack when we start talking about behaviors that are challenging. In many programs (for example, Head Start programs), there is a specific process for faculty, staff, and family members to convene as a multidisciplinary team (MDT). Their purpose is to identify behavioral concerns and specify roles and responses for everyone in the child's support team. However, in my experience, many "challenging behaviors" point directly to these instructional gaps. I have worked with teams using the "Challenging Behavior Solutions Machine" to identify and fill those gaps. You can find that approach in appendix A.

TO SPARK YOUR LEARNING... There are many outstanding resources to support educators and family members dealing with behaviors that feel challenging. Becky Bailey has devoted her career to developing a thoughtful approach called Conscious Discipline. It addresses challenging behaviors by focusing on the critical role of adult/child relationships, recognizing all that adults bring to those relationships. You can learn more about that at consciousdiscipline.com. Another organization devoted to a thoughtful approach to adult understanding of child behavior is the Brazelton Touchpoints Center (brazeltontouchpoints.org). The center advances the work of pioneering pediatrician T. Berry Brazelton. Their work focuses largely on infant and toddler issues, but many of the insights apply to preschool situations as well and all are outstanding. Finally, the National Black Child Development Institute has guided essential research in this area, helping educators see the ways that bias can creep into our understanding of what behavior is and is not appropriate. These biases directly harm young children, as seen in elevated expulsion rates for Black preschoolers, among other metrics. Learn more at nbcdi.org.

## Infant Mental Health and the Impact of Trauma on Development

Finally, one last, difficult topic. Sometimes behaviors that are challenging to adults are harder to describe and break into their component parts. They don't seem connected to school expectations and routines. They seem to come from some more complicated place in a child's life and body. And they are exhausting for even the very best teachers. Despite caring deeply for the child's well-being, you can't help but feel frustrated and defeated every day.

That's when it can be helpful to understand what the research tells us about the trauma of abuse and neglect and its impact on child development. This research is particularly relevant right now given the complex impact of the COVID-19 pandemic on the young children in our schools today. I provide a brief introduction here, but this nuanced and very complex topic deserves greater detail. If you have children in your classroom who have experienced trauma (and, sadly, it's likely that you do), seek out help. Finding resources in your community that can help you navigate the issues trauma raises will provide you with greater insight and support.

**TO SPARK YOUR LEARNING...** The Alliance for the Advancement of Infant Mental Health (allianceaimh.org) partners with state-based associations on infant mental health throughout the United States. They offer training and resources related to both general infant mental health principles and the specific needs of communities. Online, search "infant mental health" with your state name to identify the organization nearest you. Many organizations use trauma-informed care principles to support teachers working with children. Two of them are the National Center for Pyramid Model Innovations (challengingbehavior.org) and Georgetown University's Center for Early Childhood Mental Health Consultation (ecmhc.org/TTYC). The NAEYC publication by Sarah Erdman, Laura J. Colker, and Elizabeth C. Winter, *Trauma and Young Children*, and Barbara Sorrels's *Reaching and Teaching Children Exposed to Trauma* are excellent resources as well.

Children do not exist in isolation but in profound connection to all that is around them. Our work requires us to provide supportive relationships, experiences, and environments to leverage that connection toward healthy development. But this profound connection children have to what surrounds them can also result in troubling developmental issues. When children have had difficult experiences involving abuse or neglect, or when they have not had the opportunity to connect to supportive experiences, they can experience extraordinary developmental challenges in your classroom.

The field of research that focuses on these challenges to early childhood development is called *infant mental health*. Research shows that children retain the effects of difficult experiences in their brains and bodies long after the experiences have ended. We know now that these effects impact children in ways we hadn't understood before. An infant who cannot understand language can still be traumatized by family violence in another room, for example, and that harm can persist throughout their childhood.

These traumatic experiences can create gaps in children's development that may reveal themselves in surprising ways in your classroom. A child who suffered severe neglect may be very clingy one day and reject all affection the next. Another child who worked hard to please teachers for their first few weeks of preschool may, after establishing trust in the adults, suddenly burst into defiance and rage seemingly without any prompt.

Trained infant mental health professionals are adept at helping you make sense of these situations and adapt your approaches to these children. In particular, they can help you recognize the ways in which your attitude and behaviors may in fact be preventing you from providing support for some of the children in your care. Knowing the basics of early childhood development in each of the four domains (physical, cognitive, language and literacy, social and emotional), you can better identify the responses of students who may be struggling with basic expectations. When you locate such struggles, an infant mental health professional can help you be on the lookout for behaviors that don't fit your sense of what should or shouldn't be happening in your classroom. They can help you recognize what may be happening in a child's brain and body.

# Your Story as a Professional Educator and Caregiver

This chapter covered a lot! Take time to review the topics, flagging areas you want to learn more about. Then grab your journal or a piece of paper and write your answers to these reflection questions:

1. What expertise, knowledge, and insight about child development can you bring to children, colleagues, and families as an early childhood professional right now?

2. As you review the chapter, what do you think you need to learn more about to help you serve children better?

3. Are there aspects of child development that you find difficult to recognize in the behaviors of children you serve? How can you develop your skills to look for and notice those aspects?

4. What learning story do you want to tell about yourself on your journey to become the best educator and caregiver you can be?

# CHAPTER 2
# Planning and Reflection

Two decades ago, I transitioned from running a university professional development institute to being a preschool director. The most challenging part of the transition didn't involve content knowledge, instructional savvy, or interacting with teachers, children, or families. By far, the most challenging thing for me involved learning entirely new ways to approach the question of control.

In my previous position, I had gotten used to the assumption that, most of the time, I could anticipate what my day would be like. I could schedule appointments for meetings, school visits, and even extended stretches of time to work on my own. I knew that with few exceptions my planned schedule and my unfolding day would match up nicely.

I really liked those calm, orderly days! And I was pretty thrown when my new life as a preschool director made nearly all of them disappear.

Suddenly, I had to accept that my daily, weekly, and monthly plans were rough drafts at best. On any given day, I might need to devote myself to something urgent, important, and wholly unexpected. It might be a licensing visit, classroom coverage shortages, a family crisis, or, each winter, a few snowstorms! That instability meant that I had to learn how to maintain important routines, prioritize longer-range goals, and lead with a stable mindset, all while rolling with whatever punches the day would throw. I had to fundamentally change the way I understood time at work and shift my understanding of what I could and couldn't control. And I had to collaborate—with teachers, administrators, family members, state officials, even children—all day long.

I'm convinced that this situation is true for nearly every preschool educator! Running a preschool classroom involves having the ability to plan each day, week, and month with clear goals in mind. This goes hand in hand with a parallel ability to make changes at the last moment or even in the middle of activities that aren't working.

> To be the best early childhood professional you can be, you need to approach planning and reflection both as individual and as collective activities.

So, this chapter focuses on planning and reflection. To be the best early childhood professional you can be, you need to approach planning and reflection both as individual and as collective activities. As noted in principle 8, you can't do it alone, and no one can do it for you. This chapter covers some of the key points of working on your own and with your colleagues to build your professionalism. We'll consider learning how to plan intelligently, reflect productively, and create outstanding environments for both the children in your care and the adults with whom you partner.

You may be reading this book before starting your work in a preschool classroom. If so, approach this chapter as an opportunity for individual reflection in preparation for your work. Or you may already work in a preschool classroom. If that's the case, you'll be able to use the individual activities along with the group activities to benefit your team as a whole. In either case, be sure to have a pen or pencil and some paper or a work journal handy as you read. Let's get started!

## Collaborative Planning in Early Childhood Education

Most early childhood educators work with at least one other teacher in their classroom. That means that all activities in the classroom, in one way or another, involve collaboration. Let's be honest: collaboration is no easy task most of the time. Human beings are tricky, with no two of us alike. It's wonderful to think that our different perspectives could blend together harmoniously. But so often those differences can result in frustration.

We need to find ways to collaborate efficiently in our profession. But very few of us have ever had training for this essential component of our work. In higher education, most instruction on collaboration is implied, not explicit, connected to group projects or student teaching stints. Meanwhile, given the requirements of classroom coverage, it's hard to learn collaboration while at work.

To develop an effective approach to collaborative planning requires skills and the right mindset. And you'll find it helpful to keep the principles from the introduction handy as you embark on this work.

Following principle 3, prioritize honesty and transparency, cultivating trust in all that you do. Every interaction matters as you build trust. When you make a mistake, turn to principle 7 and rethink what went wrong. When the chatter turns to compliance, blame, and complaint, you need to shift to the attitude of ownership reflected in principle 9. All of this effort supports principle 8, leading with collaboration and communication, the foundation of this chapter.

In her doctoral research, Emisha Maytubby, the chair of the Family and Consumer Sciences department at Langston University, explored the complicated world of teaching teams in early childhood education. She determined that effectively functioning teaching teams better supported children's growth and development. She also identified the particular characteristics of those teams and created tools to support the cultivation of those characteristics.

In her research, Maytubby identified four specific factors that are essential to effective preschool teams. These are a shared sense of supportive collaboration; an openness to exchanging ideas; a recognition of the need to collaborate despite differences in personal style; and a commitment to putting plans into action.

You can probably see how these qualities align nicely with the principles structuring this book. A classroom characterized by these four factors would be an enjoyable place to work!

To promote these characteristics, Maytubby created a thoughtful system that documents teaching team practices and perceptions. The system helps the team communicate and collaborate more effectively. You can find a detailed overview of this approach, along with some very useful forms, in appendix B.

Improving teacher team dynamics requires some genuine leadership. Teachers often struggle giving and receiving feedback. Even though we are committed to our own growth as professionals, it's hard at times to hear constructive criticism. This is where prioritizing the principles can help. Emphasize that you are taking steps to improve collaboration and communication with positive intent. The goal is to move from blame and judgment to ownership. Explicitly commit to doing the best with the team at hand, pointing out strengths. All of these practices can lead to more conversations, building the team as you go.

**TO SPARK YOUR LEARNING...** Douglas Stone and Sheila Heen have devoted their careers to helping people participate in difficult conversations productively. In doing so, they learned that most people are quite terrible at receiving feedback. So, instead of devoting themselves to the project of giving good feedback, they shifted to the recipient. They explore how best to hear and reflect on feedback productively. In their book *Thanks for the Feedback: The Science and Art of Receiving Feedback Well* (2015), they offer thoughtful guidance on how to listen to all kinds of feedback and respond in useful ways.

Of course, facilitating the meetings described in appendix B is its own project, requiring skills that your team may not have in their toolbox. Turn to appendix C for some guidance on developing effective facilitation skills.

**TO SPARK YOUR LEARNING...** Let's face it: sometimes all the best planning and intention runs into obstacles. Here are two good resources for working through those obstacles. In *Getting Along*, Amy Gallo (2022) shares tools for recognizing the importance of work relationships even when there are challenges. Gallo identifies some of the archetypes people run into in their workplaces, and she provides guidance for making sure people protect themselves when things get really difficult. Similarly, in *Finding Your Way Through Conflict* (2020), Christine Snyder and I provide a detailed exploration of conflict in the early childhood workplace. We offer concrete strategies to help you approach conflict productively and build stronger relationships in the process.

# Collaborative Planning with Children and Families

As discussed in the first chapter, preschoolers are naturally engaged with the world around them. They are learning about phenomena, objects, symbols, themselves, and each other all day long through play. When you're planning activities, find ways to activate their interests and development. This helps create particularly engaging experiences. Children are fascinating planners-in-the-making!

There are many ways to engage children in planning, both individually and in groups. One of the classics that is used throughout elementary school is the KWL chart. This is a simple framework for focusing on a particular topic or theme. First you elicit as much information as you can from the students about what they already *Know* concerning the topic. Then you help them generate questions regarding what they *Want to know* about the topic. You gather ideas about the sorts of experiences and activities that could help them answer those questions. As you complete those activities, you document what you're learning all the while. Then you go back to the chart and collaboratively identify *what the group has Learned* about the topic.

Identifying what children know and want to know is deeply valuable. It promotes critical thinking in children by asking them to reflect on their own understanding in productive ways. It's also a form of assessment that helps you determine developmentally appropriate activities that meet them at their level. Finally, it's a great machine for thoughtful documentation and reflection. Children and their family members can see what they've learned in written, photographic, and artistic forms.

KWL charts, topic webs, and other project-based tools help make themes and topics relevant for the students you serve. Family members can be recruited into the process at different stages as well. They can help identify content and questions and, if they're available, participate in the project itself.

> Identifying what children know and want to know is deeply valuable. It promotes critical thinking in children by asking them to reflect on their own understanding in productive ways.

These project-based tools are typically used over the course of several weeks. They are part of a broader approach in preschool that takes advantage of children's curiosity and applies to many activities and experiences unfolding throughout the day. Simply wondering out loud about the natural world, social interactions, and any other experience is a form of open exploration and encourages an inquiring mindset without an end in mind. That open exploration can lead to more focused forms of exploration, generating opportunities for planning experiments, research topics, field trips, and more. Allowing children to identify both content and activities is usually guaranteed to create and maintain high levels of engagement.

**TO SPARK YOUR LEARNING...** From *Children's Interests to Children's Thinking: Using a Cycle of Inquiry to Plan Curriculum* provides an outstanding framework for activating children's wonder in planning (Broderick and Hong 2020). The authors' cycle of inquiry approach prioritizes open-ended design driven by children's interests while integrating other classroom requirements such as formal assessment. In addition, the Early Science Initiative at the National Research Council built on the K–12 Framework for Science Education, identifying key practices, concepts, and core ideas that can be activated in every preschool classroom (Greenfield, Alexander, and Frechette 2017).

Typically, when teachers incorporate preschool children in their planning, the topics tend to focus on content in the five areas collectively known as STEAM: science, technology, engineering, arts, and mathematics. But there is another area of learning critical to all preschoolers that benefits from a culture of inquiry: social, emotional, and behavioral development. Preschoolers learn from each other, so helping them see areas of success and opportunities for growth in these developmental domains cultivates expansive, rich experiences.

Planning with children around social, emotional, and behavioral development can be as simple as naming the sorts of social and emotional learning currently happening in your classroom. Then ask the question, "What are we working on?" The following areas of development are critical for preschool children: challenges with school expectations, interpersonal conflicts, learning how to enter play, understanding consent, and setting boundaries. And these developmental areas benefit from the same sort of thoughtful planning, grounded in inquiry, that can lead to deep collaborative learning. Ask family members what they're working on with their children at home—such as waiting, multistep sequences, and self-regulation. Their answers can provide even more developmentally appropriate topics to explore.

# Balancing Structure and Flexibility in Preschool

One of the biggest challenges for every early childhood classroom is embedded in the word *preschool*. On the one hand, preschool teachers are expected to help children become ready for school. In most classrooms, that means teaching skills to help students succeed in elementary classrooms that may be quite different from your own.

On the other hand, the "*pre–*" prefix makes it clear that an early childhood classroom precedes the expectations so often found in school settings. Curriculum and instruction need to prioritize earlier developmental needs than those anticipated by kindergarten.

It's not always easy to balance between these two perspectives! When expectations feel too high, recall the fundamentals of child development as they relate to both structure and flexibility.

Let's start with structure. From the earliest days of infancy, children depend on reliability: having adults who respond to their needs, routines and rituals that soothe and calm them, and regular opportunities to develop critical skills. The same need for anticipated structure is true for preschoolers. We know that preschoolers learn by watching others perform basic routines and tasks repetitively. Having repeated opportunities to try and fail at something, for example, is essential for their learning. This includes everything from running, to writing their names, to recovering from outbursts. However, what happens if adult expectations for and responses to those attempts change from day to day? The structure necessary for learning disappears, leaving children confused and frustrated.

Thoughtful planning to create these basic structures, routines, and expectations is a foundational component of every preschool classroom. It's worth noting that planning reveals adults' previously hidden classroom expectations. As the Challenging Behavior Solutions Machine (appendix A) reminds us, we often don't state what our expectations are. And we often don't create routines to help children understand and learn how to respond to our expectations.

> The importance of routines and structure is particularly powerful for children who struggle with our behavioral expectations. Preschool classrooms may be the last place where they will have the opportunity to learn how to respond to those expectations.

The importance of routines and structure is particularly powerful for children who struggle with our behavioral expectations. Preschool classrooms may be the last place where they will have the opportunity to learn how to respond to those expectations. Unfortunately, many children enter elementary classrooms where those expectations are simply expected—neither clearly stated nor taught. And for those children, early childhood educators must be particularly responsive.

Routines and structure are a critical component of every preschool classroom. But rule-bound environments where children have little choice and are forced to comply because "that's what will happen in kindergarten" betray the research and values of our field. Children need play-based ways to understand these expectations. Teachers need to approach children's growth and development with a deep respect for each individual child. And nothing destroys the joy of learning more quickly for preschoolers than a classroom that denies them opportunities for exploration, play, wonder, and autonomy.

One of the questions I often ask preschool teachers in interviews or one-on-one meetings is: "Have you ever had to drop a fully developed plan for the first week of school on the first day because it just wasn't working?" I learn a lot about someone's commitment to children's rights and autonomy in those answers! Preschool teachers need to be humble. It's essential that we be responsive to the needs and interests of children. That means we have to be ready to discard plans that don't engage them.

The ability to discard plans is one of the key skills every early childhood teacher needs in order to plan effectively. In addition, executing a plan can never distract you from emergent opportunities that stray far from the plan itself. A child who is

> Preschool teachers need to be humble. It's essential that we be responsive to the needs and interests of children. That means we have to be ready to discard plans that don't engage them.

experimenting with the viscosity of finger paints, for example, is revealing an opportunity to teach a critical sensory insight. This in-the-moment opportunity is more engaging and powerful than requiring them to complete a teacher-driven art project. A child who is hesitant to participate in a pretend-play activity you've planned is revealing the need to learn about entering into play with peers. All of these emergent opportunities for instruction and learning must take precedence over your plans. (Learn more about those opportunities in chapter 4.)

This dance between structure and flexibility flows throughout the best early childhood classrooms, despite all the things that get in the way. Here's a perfect example: for two decades I tried to find a curriculum planning tool that wasn't based on a five-day Monday-to-Friday week. It was impossible. And yet not a single preschooler I have ever met had their learning experiences structured by that adult calendar. Children are learning every day, all day, and it's our job to be ready to support that learning.

# Finding Time for Reflection and Planning

Before wrapping up this section, it's important to mention an unmentionable. We must acknowledge a fundamental truth about early childhood education that often goes unspoken but not unnoticed.

One of the ongoing challenges that every preschool teacher faces is not only what to do during planning time but how to get time for planning in the first place. Often, the day rolls along driven by classroom schedules and peppered by the various challenges that crop up each hour. Teachers can feel as if there isn't enough time for them to do required tasks, making it difficult to initiate other professional responsibilities.

And what is usually the first thing that gets crossed off the list? *Planning time.*

Planning and reflection are important in everything we do, and the lack of time for those activities is one of our profession's fundamental structural limitations. You may sometimes feel that it's a sign of your inability to solve what seems like a very simple problem. But that's a misunderstanding. My career has been filled with amazing educators in both classrooms and administration. And literally everyone I know finds it challenging to manage their time in preschool settings. Every. Single. Person.

Time management is one of the aspects of our profession for which we receive little training. And, in some situations, we may receive little support. So it's important for us to learn the basics of time management individually. And we must learn how to make the case for planning and reflection time.

One useful framework for time management is the Urgent/Important chart. As a school director, I put this chart on the door of my office. When someone would knock on my door to raise an issue, we would quickly determine where their situation fell on the chart. It's a simple tool for determining how and when to tackle an issue.

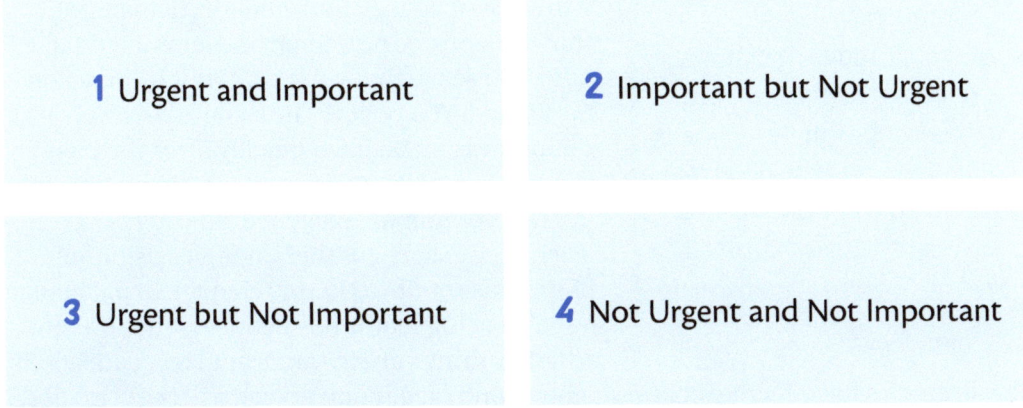

**1** Urgent and Important

**2** Important but Not Urgent

**3** Urgent but Not Important

**4** Not Urgent and Not Important

Walking through the four quadrants with any given issue, it's easy to become aware of ways that human nature drives us in one direction or another. Indeed, our culture rewards short attention spans and feels more and more like a game of *Whac-A-Mole* each day. It will take some commitment and practice to prioritize your time effectively!

Quadrant 1 is straightforward. If someone knocks on my door and says that they smelled smoke in the back corridor, the situation is both urgent and important—no argument there. It demands my attention immediately. Items in quadrant 4 are also pretty easy to spot. So many things can distract us from more productive ways to use our time. Simply noting that an issue is neither important nor urgent can free us from getting stuck in distractions. After all, there are always more pressing matters deserving our valuable time.

Meanwhile, quadrant 3 can be tricky. Disagreeing about whether something is important is one of the most common ways that people get stuck in conflict. People usually can agree about whether or not an issue is urgent. But people can easily disagree about that issue's importance given their own perspectives. What's worse, they can start to feel as if there are fundamental disagreements in the values and principles of the people involved. Those disagreements add a lot of heat and not much light!

Here's an example. You walk into your classroom at the beginning of the day ready to go. Immediately, one of your colleagues points out that the signs on the door haven't been laminated and are curling and getting torn as children arrive. It's urgent in the sense that it is happening now and could get worse. It therefore requires some attention at the moment—everyone agrees on that. But is it important?

> Children, families, and your colleagues may not recognize the importance of devoting time to planning and reflection, so you need to prioritize and advocate for that yourself.

You listen to your colleague describe the situation with a lot of energy and emotion, demanding that the signs be reprinted and laminated *right now*. You sense that your perceptions may not be aligned. You believe the issue is relatively minor and can be fixed quickly after the busy arrival time ends. These sorts of disagreements are facts of human existence. So you need to learn how to sort out these matters using some of the skills outlined in this chapter. In particular, good working teams have conversations about whether things are in quadrant 1 or quadrant 3. The strategies for effective communication and facilitation above are useful in these conversations. But those skills can only be effective if you're able to identify what issues provoke these differences of judgment.

In many ways, the most important feature of the chart involves quadrant 2. Preschool workdays are filled with urgent items, and distinguishing where to allocate your attention is ongoing work. But being stuck in quadrants 1, 3, and 4 is precisely what drains time and attention away from quadrant 2. It's how the planning can gets kicked down the road, over and over again.

For that reason, it's critical to find ways to carve out time for the important tasks of planning and reflection even when they don't feel urgent. Required curriculum plans and assessment forms that are past their due date feel urgent, for sure. But reflecting thoughtfully on your assessments and building effective curricula rarely feel as important as they should. Yet those are the beating heart of every good early childhood classroom.

That's why you need to devote time each week to quadrant 2. Children, families, and your colleagues may not recognize the importance of devoting time to planning and reflection, so you need to prioritize and advocate for that yourself.

# Knowing Your Circles of Change and Control

Finding time for planning and staying focused when you meet with your team both require complicated consideration. You must understand what power and autonomy you have as an educator in your particular workplace. When we wrote our book on conflict, Christine Snyder and I shared a tool we use to help understand two zones of activity. One zone detailed those things that we could control and change. The other zone detailed things that we didn't control and likely couldn't change.

It's a useful tool for you to consider on your own and for your team to use as a group reflection opportunity. By thinking about these issues in general, you'll have better insights for approaching the specific, related issues that arise day-to-day. You can develop a sense of acceptance about what you cannot control while focusing your energy on what you can.

Let's take a look at this approach within the framework of our principles. We'll emphasize honesty and transparency (principle 3), and we'll acknowledge that we'll try to do our best with what we've got (principle 6). Finally, we'll do our best to adopt the attitude of principle 9, moving from compliance to ownership. All early childhood programs demand that we figure out how to make expectations live authentically in our classroom. This is a core professional responsibility for every early childhood educator.

An example of the tool is shown on page 64.

## What We Can't Change or Control

Let's start with what's outside the circle. Many of the rules and expectations listed there are basic requirements. These are imposed by governmental organizations, district or organizational policies, licensing agencies, and so on. By far, the biggest one of these items involves teacher-student ratios and group size. In our profession, adults are unable to move within different workspaces throughout their day unless other adults take their place. That's a requirement that doesn't exist in many other professions. Ratio and group size may be different for different ages, in different states, and at different moments of the day, but they are critical elements outside your control that you have to follow no matter what.

Understanding your school's approach to coverage for group size and ratio is critical for you to be able to plan individually and as a team. Some schools prioritize this planning regularly. However, many do not routinely offer time for planning, especially outside of the classroom and away from children. If the constraints of ratio prevent such planning time, you must find ways to prioritize planning as a team throughout the day. Recognizing what you cannot change allows you to determine ways to

CUSTODIAL CONTRACTS

ROOM SIZE

ARRIVAL/DEPARTURE TIMES

PAY AND BENEFITS

GROUP SIZE

## Things We Cannot Change

### Things We Can Change

SCHEDULES

TEACHER/FAMILY RELATIONS

SELF-CARE OUTSIDE OF HERE

ACTIVITIES

PARENTS SEEING US AS PROFESSIONALS

ATTITUDE

ROUTINES

KNOWLEDGE AND TECHNIQUES

EFFORT WE PUT INTO RELATIONSHIPS

FINDING JOY

COMMUNITY PARTNERSHIPS

### In Our Control

COMPLIANCE

### Outside Our Control

CHILD NEEDS

CALENDAR

CONSTANT TRANSITIONS

HIGHER ED

meet your goals and accept the limitations. Tackling this challenge as a team helps everyone feel engaged and valued in these critical planning activities.

The faculty and staff at my school wanted to keep an eye on these complex issues of control and change. It was no surprise that many of the things that nagged us throughout the year were on our version of the diagram! So it was very useful to return to it when needed; that made us familiar with the characteristics and complications of the things on our list. Having already considered them thoughtfully made the specific frustrations less potent—though, of course, it didn't erase those frustrations completely.

For example, although our school had a wonderful custodian during the day, over the years we dealt with a series of less-than-outstanding custodians in the evenings. We often found unpleasant surprises when we arrived in the morning that made us want to change the contracts. But we had no control over custodial contracts despite their environmental importance. You will have your own particular, nagging elements that belong outside the circle!

## What Is Outside Your Circle of Control?

Now it's your turn. Get a piece of blank paper and draw a circle that covers about half the page. Outside of that circle, write the sorts of things that you cannot change and that are outside of your control as an early childhood educator. Write anything that comes to mind; don't censor yourself.

Next, take a look at the principles we've been embracing in this book. Think about how you might shift your attitude for yourself, your colleagues, the children you serve, and their families in approaching these issues. That is to say, you can always change your attitude, and doing so is contagious. What's more, accepting these constraints might help you see opportunities, allowing you to pivot into a more positive stance. Approaching challenges with an opportunity mindset can turn lemons into lemonade!

To that end, here's one last set of questions. Look at the items that are outside the circle and ask yourself: *Are these really outside my control? Is it true that they can never change? What would it take to make such changes?* After all, everything on this chart was created by humans!

There are often procedures in place to promote such changes on a regular basis. States review licensing requirements all the time, providing opportunities for public comment on drafts and inviting testimonials from educators at hearings. Similarly, policies within a high-quality organization can be improved by thoughtful feedback. And if you believe that there are things that are simply unjust in your workplace, you may well have a moral obligation to voice those concerns.

It might take a while, and it won't always work. But are there places where you might work individually or in groups to improve some of the things that are getting in the way?

## What We Can Change and Control

Now let's take a look at the inside of the circle, filled with lots of things that can be modified, adjusted, and otherwise changed. Many things inside the circle are basic elements of preschool classroom life that we will discuss in future chapters: routines, schedules, family engagement activities, and so on. When most preschool teachers think about planning on the job, these are the required tasks they expect. They can do many of them individually or within their classroom team.

Other requirements are often trickier because we can't do them on our own or with our classroom team—they take broader collaboration. For example, in one program, we had mixed-age infant/toddler classrooms. Children transitioned on their third birthdays into preschool classrooms. Supporting these children's transitions was often confusing. It required the child and the family to interact not only with the infant/toddler team that they had gotten to know well but also with an entirely new preschool classroom team. Meanwhile, trying to ensure the two classroom teams had the proper ratio of adults to children was always a challenge!

This approach can only work if at least one person makes a commitment to changing their attitude, viewing a tricky challenge as an opportunity. That's why several of the items inside the circle involve our own individual connection to a situation instead of an external challenge. We have lots of control over our own connections and behaviors.

Attitude is not the same as mood. Attitude is a choice, something you can decide you are going to change for the better, each moment of each day. It takes practice, but finding possibility and genuine joy in difficult situations is a great skill to have as an early childhood educator, especially for the pessimists!

Figuring out how to approach these challenges as opportunities involves effort, to be sure. But Harvard University professor Robert Waldinger, the coauthor of the biggest study on happiness in history, reminds us that human connection is our superpower (Waldinger and Schulz 2023). What you invest in relationships comes back amplified, creating better educational opportunities for children and families and a better workplace for you and your colleagues. So why not lead the way?

Now it's your turn—and this time, let's use the "What? So What? Now What?" process to get to the heart of the matter. Get out your paper again and ask yourself: *What are the things that I can change? What things are at least partly within my control?* Write anything that comes to mind. Label each item with an "I" for things that are entirely individual or a "C" for things that are partly or wholly collaborative.

Next, take another sheet of paper. Look at each individual item on your list and ask yourself: *So what? Why is this important? What would changing this improve?* Imagine you're explaining this to yourself in your journal. Try to treat this issue as an opportunity to make things better. What would you say to your best self?

> What you invest in relationships comes back amplified, creating better educational opportunities for children and families and a better workplace for you and your colleagues. So why not lead the way?

Do the same for each item that you identified as collaborative. Imagine that you are raising this as an opportunity with other people on your team. Why is this a good opportunity to work on something that really matters?

Finally, ask yourself: *Now what? What steps can I take to make these changes happen?* Depending on how long your list is, it may be very daunting to identify steps for every single thing inside that circle! So break them down into three groups.

- Pick a few that you can change tomorrow. Really! Identify some things that are completely in your control and that you can just decide you're going to approach differently when you come to work. Where can you make an attitude adjustment?

- Then pick a few things to which you can devote time and effort over the next week or two. Again, start small. Consider one that you could pursue with a colleague, trying to build those human connections in treating challenges as opportunities.

- Finally, pick one or two things that will require a couple of months of collaborative work to really shift. These require heavy lifting and the muscles of other humans! So be sure to build up your own and your team's capacity for this collaboration with some smaller, less-taxing successes.

Exercises connected to the change/control chart are valuable to do both individually and with your team on a regular basis. They don't have to be a big production. For example, you and your team could keep your chart handy and review it every couple of months to figure out what's changed. This is a great way to keep your eye on the foundational planning and reflection that is required to do the rest of your work as an early childhood professional.

**TO SPARK YOUR LEARNING...** Simon Sinek wrote a tremendously popular book based on these same principles. In *Start with Why: How Great Leaders Inspire Everyone to Take Action* (2011), he encourages readers to approach the "What? So What? Now What?" questions using his Golden Circle, a variation on these three questions. He's got several YouTube videos, including a TED Talk. Check him out!

## Moving from Compliance to Ownership

These challenging exercises present you with an opportunity to think carefully about principle 9. Early childhood educators work in highly regulated environments with a whole host of requirements and expectations. You are likely to think many make perfect sense, but odds are you'll find some burdensome and disagreeable. No matter where you work or what kind of program you work in, this high level of regulation is an undeniable fact of early childhood education and care. And it's no abstraction: this regulation will show up in various ways throughout your workday and will never disappear. As a result, becoming an outstanding early childhood professional requires that you find a way to accept this reality.

We provide many hours of care and education each day for groups of human beings who cannot answer basic questions about what happened. Preverbal infants and toddlers don't have the language or other communication tools to tell us about their day. Preschoolers are just figuring out basic concepts about time, causality, and narrative. The young children we serve cannot tell us when their needs have been ignored. They can't express when their rights have been violated or their dignity has been harmed.

These developmental facts mean that, as early childhood professionals, we must do our work in settings that impose a lot of structure and control on nearly everything we do. Consider room design, food service, naptime, curriculum selection and implementation, furniture, documentation, playground design, and so on. Regulations that structure our work reflect the expectations we have as the adults responsible for the children we serve, children who cannot speak to that responsibility.

Working in a field that doesn't receive nearly as much respect as it deserves, we may find a lot of these regulations themselves to be disrespectful. They seem to be proof of a lack of trust. That makes a lot of emotional sense, especially after a long day when someone points out a regulation we missed or task we fumbled! So it's good to remember principle 10 when we're talking about such issues. Placing the child at the center and viewing the classroom from their perspective can help us pivot and remember why our profession has so many rules.

Of course, merely putting up with regulations is not enough. We need to activate principle 9 and shift from treating those regulations with a *compliance mindset* to approaching them with an *ownership mindset*.

> The young children we serve cannot tell us when their needs have been ignored. They can't express when their rights have been violated or their dignity has been harmed.

When we are in a compliance mindset, we perform tasks and activities to comply with what someone else is telling us to do. It doesn't really matter whether what we're doing is important. It doesn't matter whether we even agree with it, and at times we may deeply disagree with it! We're just doing what we're told. We have no sense of the value of doing something or the consequences of not doing something.

Often, when we're in a compliance mindset, we are looking for villains to blame. It may be an instructional coach who doesn't recognize our special qualities and is focusing on a performance gap. Or perhaps it's a licensing specialist who caught us on a "bad day." Maybe it's a director or principal who asks about late assessment paperwork. When we're in a compliance mindset, it's very easy to treat these people—professionals who are trying to do their jobs—as our nemeses. They are the problem; it's certainly not us.

When we are in an ownership mindset, we are deeply aware of the *why*. We understand the reason an expectation is important and has value regardless of our opinion about it. In an ownership mindset, we shift responsibility away from some external nemesis and back to ourselves. Instructional coaches exist to help us identify ways to improve our instruction. Licensing specialists are paid to make sure that the state has authorized a program that is taking seriously its statutes and laws. A director or principal provides documentation to funders, government, and families. They also assemble information to review what is working in a program and what needs further support.

In other words, we see all of these people as professionals like us. We realize they are doing their best to perform their roles in service of the community's children and families. We recognize the reason why these expectations exist, even if we disagree with them, and that frees us from the nasty blame game. We braid together principle 9 with principle 6, moving into ownership and committing to doing our best in the situation at hand.

One final note. Ownership does not mean being silent when it's time to address concerns, fix inadequate procedures, and address systemic injustices. Quite the opposite: we respond to the current expectations of the early childhood system while at the same time advocating for necessary improvements, with our equity lens in hand. And every time we do that, we have to keep the child at the center of our considerations.

> When we are in an ownership mindset, we are deeply aware of the *why*. We understand the reason an expectation is important and has value regardless of our opinion about it.

So take a moment now, and take a deep breath, and create two lists. Use these questions for the first list: Which required aspects of the work do you approach in a mode of compliance? Which do you find annoying or stupid, and maybe sometimes even let slide? For the second list, write down the requirements that make sense to you, the expectations that you are happy to own. What's on that list?

Now, placing the child at the center, jot down some notes about the *why* for both lists. Looking at the expectations you happily own, what is the importance of those expectations? Why do they exist? What value do they have? Now ask yourself the same questions about the compliance mindset items. Why are they important? What value do they have?

Finally—and perhaps you need another deep breath here!—take a moment to consider the possibility of embracing some of those compliance expectations with an ownership mindset. What would it take to shift your attitude about one or two of these requirements? And what would the benefits be for your colleagues, the children, the families, and yourself?

## Reflection Is Not Optional!

All of the work you do as an early childhood professional requires regular reflection. And that starts with yourself. In order to make principle 6 come alive and do your best with what you've got, you need to make sure you have a deep understanding of who you are. After all, *you* are, at the most basic level, what you've got!

Who you are has a profound impact on all the interpersonal relations that make your work possible. And principle 2 is based on the science of child development: every interaction matters, so you need to have a good understanding of yourself if you want to make every interaction matter.

Arriving at that self-understanding takes work, and there are no simple solutions. Over the years, I've heard many educators talk about the need to "leave their problems at the door," as if their problems can be packed up while they walk from the parking lot to the school entrance. Unfortunately, most of us have challenges that can't be packed up so neatly and quickly. So instead of using invisible luggage that might burst open, we turn to other, more useful ideas about reflecting as an early childhood professional. These perspectives don't pretend we can leave parts of ourselves at the door.

At the Center for Early Education and Development (CEED) at the University of Minnesota, researchers have been exploring ways that early childhood professionals can create dialogues to help themselves reflect on their work with children and families. Known as *reflective supervision*, these dialogues emphasize the importance of reflection in supervisory relationships.

One of the key concepts of effective reflection involves developing self-understanding and enacting it in the workplace. CEED calls this *professional use of self*. Instead of asking what parts of ourselves we want to leave out, we ask how different components of our identities, experiences, and expertise can be activated in our work as professionals. We don't treat ourselves as accidents waiting to happen, carrying around problems that we need to dump at the door to prevent us from screwing things up. We treat ourselves as resources that we can use intelligently and mindfully. After all, we are professionals in a field based on human interaction.

**TO SPARK YOUR LEARNING...** The Center for Early Education and Development has many tools available for individuals and groups interested in exploring concepts such as the professional use of self, which you can access at ceed.umn.edu/professional-development. They have also created a Reflective Interaction Observation Scale (RIOS™) that can help you determine more effective ways to practice reflective supervision.

Of course, for you to activate those components of yourself, you need to practice thoughtful self-reflection on an ongoing basis. Many early childhood professionals do this in their journals in regular writing assignments they don't share with anyone. They explore what matters to them and what is frustrating, where their successes unfold and where problems crop up. Others find colleagues they can interact with in a shared reflection. They avoid blame, criticism, and guilt and instead emphasize the importance of activating the qualities that brought them to the field in the first place.

Whatever process you use, it's critical to reflect regularly on your own professional use of self. Use the exercises described above as well as questions like these:

- Why did you choose this field?

- What matters to you each day?

- When you have had a "good day," what happened? How can you make that happen more often?

- When you have had a "bad day," what happened? How can you make that happen less often?

- What aspects of yourself shine most brightly when things are going well? How can you activate those when things are challenging?

- Which of the ten principles are you finding easiest to enact right now? And which ones are most challenging?

# Cultivating Yourself as a Leader

Before we wrap up this chapter on planning and reflection, I want to highlight the importance of one particular form of self-reflection: thinking about yourself as a leader. This perspective may require a significant attitude shift for you. But I've learned over several decades that often the best leaders don't think of themselves as leaders.

This is particularly true in early childhood education. We usually think that leaders in schools are the people at the top of the hierarchy, the directors, principals, and administrators who are in charge. But there are many other leaders throughout every school. That's because leadership is more about an attitude than a formal position.

In *The Leap to Leader*, Adam Bryant identifies three familiar ways that leaders stand out. First, they are clear about what matters to them; they recognize and live their values and principles in ways that others can clearly perceive. (To echo Simon Sinek, they know and communicate their "why.") Second, they are clear, transparent, and skillful in making decisions. They know how to prioritize different challenges and obtain input from others to address them. Finally, they are committed to a reflective stance so that they are able to build self-awareness (Bryant 2023).

Doesn't that sound a lot like what we've been discussing so far? Early childhood professionals lean into the values and principles of our field. We put children and families first, and we make decisions based on research and best practices to support children's learning and growth. To do that, we must make dozens of decisions every day. We take input from colleagues, families, and the children in front of us not just with formal assessment practices but in many informal ways. And we know that all of our interactions with children require us to be self-aware, using our professional sense of self to support the work we are deeply committed to.

Put differently: *outstanding early childhood professionals are already leaders*. We just don't always realize it.

There are many books devoted to leadership development both in general and in early childhood specifically. Here are five suggestions for you to consider exploring on your own leadership journey.

- Raymond M. Kethledge and Michael S. Erwin make a strong case for individual self-reflection in *Lead Yourself First: Inspiring Leadership Through Solitude* (2017). They look at a wide range of leaders who gained strength through solitude, and they identify ways to cultivate clarity, creativity, emotional balance, and moral courage.

- In *Graceful Leadership in Early Childhood Education* (2018), early childhood educator Ann McClain Terrell shares her own powerful story about transitioning through leadership stages to become an ever-more-capable and effective leader. She weaves her narrative with theories of leadership and practical advice, and she demonstrates the importance of grace and dignity in addressing the challenges and hurdles of our profession.

- Brené Brown has written several books that encourage everyone to, as her 2018 book declares, *Dare to Lead*. In this book, Brown explores the ways that some human traits that we typically think of as negative are actually sources of strength, and she encourages us to lean into our vulnerability to become better leaders. She emphasizes how living into our values helps us cultivate trust as a form of courage and bravery and expand our skills in conversations, interactions, and our work.

- Living into our values in concrete ways is at the core of *Leading Anti-Bias Early Childhood Programs: A Guide to Change, for Change* by Louise Derman-Sparks, Debbie LeeKeenan, and John Nimmo (2023). Three leaders in the effort to promote anti-bias education in our profession, the authors advance the principles and guidelines that are the foundation of this commitment. They offer ways to approach children, colleagues, and families with these principles in hand.

- Though she comes from the world of technology, Kim Scott has many useful things to share with early childhood educators in her book *Radical Candor: How to Get What You Want by Saying What You Mean* (2019). By communicating clearly and honestly, not just in terms of expressing yourself but also in terms of listening and interacting, you can build "radically candid relationships," just the sort that can be most powerful in your preschool classroom.

Finally, take encouragement from one of the most astute groups of leaders on the planet: preschoolers themselves. One of the joys of working in a preschool classroom is that the majority of the humans in the room are committed to honesty and transparency and will prioritize those values while sacrificing almost everything else. Preschoolers usually tell it like it is. They haven't learned all the complicated social rules about what you should and shouldn't say. Instead, they let you know exactly what's on their minds.

For example, one key leadership trait involves mentioning the unmentionables. This practice is particularly true when you are embracing principle 4. Getting out your equity lens often means taking a close look at things that adults find uncomfortable to discuss and would rather not explore. But preschool classrooms usually have one or two dozen children who are completely committed to mentioning the unmentionables! They state the obvious and the not-so-obvious, making sure you know what they're thinking on a regular basis. They notice what's fair and unfair. They remember what you said you were going to do yesterday when you are failing to do it today. They may not have the sophistication to know how to use it, but they certainly possess Kim Scott's radical candor.

**TO SPARK YOUR LEARNING...** The *Harvard Business Review* (*HBR*; hbr.org) provides thoughtful, research-based information about many topics in leadership. You can subscribe to their journal for a fee, but each month they offer a couple of free articles to nonsubscribers. In addition, *HBR* provides fantastic, free daily email newsletters on topics such as leadership, group facilitation, communication, and much more.

# Your Story as a Professional Educator and Caregiver

Review the topics covered in this chapter. Then grab your journal or a piece of paper and write your answers to these three reflection questions:

1. What expertise, knowledge, and insight about planning and reflection can you bring to children, families, and colleagues as an early childhood professional right now?

2. As you review the chapter, what do you think you need to learn more about to help you serve children better?

3. What learning story do you want to tell about yourself on your journey to become the best educator and caregiver you can be?

# CHAPTER 3
# Room Design and Materials Planning

## A Thought Experiment

Before we get to the details of room design and materials, let's do a thought experiment. Grab a sheet of paper and a pen or pencil, and take a look at the photo below.

Write some answers to the following questions.

- What are blocks?
- What happens in the block area?
- What is important about blocks?

Turn the page *after* you've written a response for each question.

Now take a look at these photos:

On the other side of your sheet of paper, write some answers to those same questions.

- What are blocks?

- What happens in the block area?

- What is important about blocks?

Now compare the two responses. What do you notice about the differences prompted by these photographs?

I have facilitated this activity for dozens of teachers over the years, so I predict that your written responses may be something like this. Responding to the first photo, teachers say that blocks are discrete shapes that are assembled in particular ways to build organized, stable structures. Children enact multistep decisions in the block area about their building. They make plans, execute them, and complete their tasks. Blocks are important because they support STEAM concepts involving shape, space, physics, and so on. Blocks support individual children in their individual development of those skills.

When I show the second and third photos, teachers usually laugh out loud. It's because they catch themselves—they realize that they bought into the somewhat academic fantasy depicted in the first photo. It shows an isolated child posing with his complex, perfect structure. The entire proud moment is captured perfectly, frozen in time. When I ask teachers if they've ever seen anything remotely like the first image in their own classrooms, they laugh again. They assure me that the photograph has absolutely nothing to do with their experiences.

Meanwhile, looking at the second and third photos, teachers immediately point out that they show "the real world" of a classroom. So what is it about those photos that feels so real?

For starters, unlike the first photo, they do not show a single child with his finished structure. Instead, the photos depict a sprawling group of children interacting together in activity that spills across the shared space. There seem to be a few independent workers here and there. But most children are interacting in small groups, moving from one section of a shared, unfolding project to another.

The structures they build are beautiful and creative in their own ways. But let's face it: unlike the castle in the first photo, none of the structures are adult masterpieces that would pass muster from a contractor, architect, or urban planner. Instead, they are clearly children's masterpieces, full of energy and creativity, unconstrained by adult standards of perfection.

Finally, unlike the static first photo, the second and third photos capture movement. This quality is, I think, what makes the photographs seem more "real." The children's playful interactions flow through the space. In these more social depictions of block play, children negotiate plans, test out initial steps, note successes and failures, and renegotiate plans. Structures grow, change, fall, and grow again. The entire organic enterprise is more like a living ecosystem. Blocks are the oxygen that keeps the energy high, and the children never arrive at a photo-ready, finished product that is "done."

When we talk about room design and materials, we want to make sure we are talking about the real world of the second and third photographs and not the static fantasy world of the first. Sure, at times a child might build a wonderful structure ready for *Architectural Digest*. And children are certainly using their geometric and spatial skills, multistep reasoning, and core science concepts in any building endeavor. But in the real world, activity in the block area—indeed, in every area of the classroom— means something far more wide-ranging, engaging, and joyful.

## Learning/Activity Areas

Clearly defined learning and activity areas that provide readily accessible, play-based opportunities for children are essential components of every preschool classroom. Indeed, the classroom environment is your teaching partner. And as the designer of that environment, you are responsible for every aspect of the space. That means identifying the basic building blocks of the classroom, adjusting for the design and limitations of the space you have, and populating learning areas with engaging, appropriate learning materials.

There are many different approaches to determining exactly what learning areas are required. For example, the Early Learning Division at the Oregon Department of Education lists the following ten required areas (2022, 195):

- Blocks
- Manipulatives
- Books
- Sensory experiences
- Gross motor activities
- Music
- Art
- Dramatic play
- Science/exploration
- Discovery of nature

This slightly different list of required areas comes from Head Start of Lane County, Oregon (2013, para. 3).

- Blocks/Building (may be in Circle area)
- Dramatic Play
- Tabletop Activities (Toys and Games)
- Sensory Table
- Creative Arts
- Literacy (Writing Table, Library, Listening, Computer)
- Discovery (Science and Math)
- Circle (Music and Movement)
- Quiet Area

Talk to your administrator to determine what local, state, or program guidelines require. But whatever those requirements are, there are a few general principles to keep in mind as you build these areas.

First, consider how preschool bodies will inhabit the space. What do you need to do to make their experiences successful and safe? Principle 10 is particularly handy in this regard. When you imagine what it would be like to be in a preschooler's body, what do you see? Is the space easy to get into and out of? How many small humans can successfully participate at once? Are the materials accessible and visible? Are the children who are using the space also accessible and visible?

Next, consider the room layout, starting with boundaries and traffic flow. For example, a block area with no firm boundaries next to a major thoroughfare is likely to create problems when traffic flows right through a carefully built structure. On the other hand, a dramatic play area might benefit from more open access—allowing children to enter and leave the restaurant operating there with ease. And identifying a quiet space in a boisterous classroom may be trickier than you think!

Layout also requires carefully considering how each area will be organized, used, and cleaned up. Here are a few considerations for particular areas:

- **Sensory experiences and art areas** require two absolutely essential elements. If you forget them, you'll be reminded moments after opening those areas up! First, they require flooring that is extremely easy to clean. It should be easy to sweep up sand, paper scraps, broken crayons, and other dry materials and easy to wipe up cookie dough, goop, paint, and other wet messes. But the floor isn't the only thing that will be messy! So place these areas right next to a children's sink outfitted with soap and paper towels that are easy to access.

- **The blocks area** needs shelving for the blocks; a flat, level floor that provides a firm foundation for building; and carpet to muffle the sounds of structural collapses.

- **Science and manipulatives areas** require a table, a few chairs, and excellent lighting. Transparent containers for manipulatives need short sides that allow small hands and wrists to reach into them.

- **The library** needs low bookshelves resting on the floor with several rows to provide a wide array of inviting titles. Outfit it with carpet and comfortable furniture, not only for individual children but for you to convene a small group for an impromptu reading.

- **Music and dramatic play areas** need efficient storage systems for costumes, equipment, and instruments. They also require lots of space for the spontaneous and planned dance parties you'll hold there!

As you draft each component of your design, take very good notes on exactly how you will teach children to play and learn in that activity area. Keep asking yourself: *Are my expectations developmentally appropriate? What specific direct instruction, role-modeling, role-playing, and co-playing will I provide?* Determining exactly how you will teach children to function in those spaces will force you to consider children's social and emotional skills, temperaments, and interest levels. All of these are critical components of good design.

Finally, recognize that any design you decide on is likely to change once children inhabit it! Flexibility is key—and essential for your sanity. Indeed, what may at first look like behavioral issues could be linked to design problems that are far more easily fixed. Watch for signs that an area may be ready for a design overhaul: conflict among children during play, squabbling about cleanup and organization, misplaced or hard-to-find items, even your sore back. And remember: the children in your classroom are probably outstanding design collaborators! Be sure to include them in the process.

# Design Questions to Consider

In reading this chapter, embrace your inner designer. That might mean making the shift from thinking of classrooms as static, neat, controlled spaces to classrooms as flowing, vital, open-ended environments for learning. A high-quality classroom welcomes all children and promotes all of their developmental needs by activating connectedness, exploration, and wonder. Here are some questions to consider as you plan for room design and classroom materials.

## What Are the *Why* and the *How*?

To get started, it's time to get out our "What? So What? Now What?" framework. It's fun to snoop through catalogs of learning materials but easy to get stuck on the *what*, too focused on the space and the objects within it. So in room design, start with the next question: So what? What are the developmental goals you have for the children in your care? And what spaces or materials serve those needs best?

When pondering these questions, be sure to use the whole developmental range of children, across all areas discussed in chapter 1. Don't get stuck in any one developmental category. After all, every object and space in your classroom will activate a number of different developmental areas. Take each of them into consideration as you design.

In addition, as you'll read in chapter 4, your instructional strategies will always include activating every developmental skill, regardless of the area children are in. Literacy doesn't happen only in the writing area, and the entire classroom is the "social/emotional development area." And review the second and third photographs above (page 78): how many developmental domains are flowing through those playful interactions?

Of course, children can only build their skills within those developmental domains if the context and materials engage them meaningfully. This requires you to ask the foundational question about developmentally appropriate practice: Now what? When deciding to build a particular learning space and stock it with specific materials, ask yourself: *How exactly will children use this space and these materials? Which children will engage those objects in that space? And which children will not or cannot?* There's no benefit to children if the room and its contents are inaccessible. A roomful of disengaged preschoolers makes for a long day for teachers!

The question of use is also an equity question. Are there certain groups of children for whom an activity is more or less meaningful? This could be due to issues related to identity, culture, community, and so on. Consider photographs that depict only boys and men in certain professional roles; art materials that don't include the full range of skin tones found in your classroom; or dance parties using music with lyrics only in English. It's critical to

> When deciding to build a particular learning space and stock it with specific materials, ask yourself: *How exactly will children use this space and these materials? Which children will engage those objects in that space? And which children will not or cannot?*

be aware of the ways that seemingly benign decisions can exclude and marginalize children without any intent on your part to do so.

Finally, it is important to ask the *why* and the *how* when using technology. There's no question that children need to understand the basics of our rapidly changing world, and that includes developing an understanding of how computers work, what the internet is for, and so on. That said, all too often the *why* of a computer in a preschool classroom seems more about babysitting and distraction than learning, with some children engaging more than others.

**TO SPARK YOUR LEARNING...** The National Association for the Education of Young Children, in collaboration with the Fred Rogers Center, created a helpful position statement on the use of technology and other interactive media. It's a deep dive into the *why* and *how* of these powerful tools. Read more at naeyc.org/resources/topics/technology-and-media.

## How Much Stuff Is "Just Right"?

Like Goldilocks, your job as a preschool teacher is to approach classroom design and materials selection by trying to find that "just right" place. A quality classroom provides enough stimulation to engage children's playful learning but not so much that children are confused or overwhelmed. Of course, as principle 5 reminds us, "just right" will be different for every classroom, teaching team, and group of children. There is no one-size-fits-all answer.

As you plan, you have to think about the lively, flowing learning environment as a whole instead of focusing on each individual item or decision. Each poster, photograph, art project, bit of learning documentation, and parent newsletter may well be appropriate on its own. But when combined in your classroom, what environment do they create for each child?

Addressing this question requires being very honest about some choices, even if we made them with good intentions. Let's take the importance of print-rich environments. There is no question that children in preschool benefit from opportunities to engage with print in multiple areas throughout the day. But a classroom with twenty-two alphabets and five number lines on the walls isn't a classroom that is using print in thoughtful, engaging ways. (I've been in that classroom, and I counted!) Though well-intended, this design may be overwhelming, and not only for adults like you and me who can read and write. Preliterate children who find this swirl of letters and numbers incomprehensible are likely to experience the environment as a barrier, not a path, to learning.

Finally, asking yourself how much stuff is "just right" demands that you confront your desire for decor. Aside from required adult items like family notices and fire drill directions, everything in the classroom must be connected to children's learning, either as something to engage children in a learning experience or as documentation of a past learning experience. Everything else is merely decoration and needs to go.

> A quality classroom provides enough stimulation to engage children's playful learning but not so much that children are confused or overwhelmed.

So as you walk through that education supply store or flip through the pages of a preschool materials catalog, ask yourself what learning experience or community value you are promoting. And if you are in an existing preschool classroom, look around. Ask yourself, *Do I really use this to promote children's learning and growth? Or do I just kind of like the way it looks?* Chances are that, with some honest reflection, you will create a room that is "just right"—and spend a whole lot less money!

## How Will I Teach Children How to Use the Spaces and Materials?

A child tosses a book across the floor, causing a teacher to bark, "That's not how we treat our books!" The teacher places the book back on the bookshelf, after which the child does the same thing again. Another child stands outside the dramatic play area, silently watching three engaged children prepare food in the kitchen to serve on a table. The onlooker is unsure of what to do. Yet another child, also watching the dramatic play, raises a cup of finger paint to her lips with a smile. The teacher panics and shouts her name, causing the child to drop the cup, cover her face with her paint-smeared hands, and start to sob.

If you've ever spent time in another country, eating a meal where the food culture is different from your own, or found yourself expected to follow rules you knew nothing about, perhaps you can sympathize with these three children! There are elements of your classroom that feel exactly like a foreign country to children. That means that every time you add a new area or element, it needs to be introduced and explained. Children need to learn how to interact with materials and each other in your classroom.

Let's take the three children in the paragraph above. We know that many children grow up in homes that do not have regular access to books, sometimes because the adults in those homes cannot read. It's entirely possible that those children do not know the rules for handling books. Some may never have held one.. Meanwhile, if their homes are filled with balls and other objects you toss around with your family members, it would make sense they would test the projectile qualities of books!

As for the child observing the kitchen activity, we know that entering into play is an extraordinarily complicated act. Participation requires children to understand the rules of interaction among their peers so that they can follow them. To make things even more challenging, a dramatic play setup does not always mirror a child's own home environment. Finally, many children experience food insecurity, and they may not have seen food prepared in that way at all. Many families of all economic levels do not have adults who cook meals from scratch and serve them seated at a table.

> Instead of assuming children have the experience, knowledge, and skills to engage effectively in your classroom, consider each element of your design and ask: *How will I teach the use of this object or area?*

Finally, the tears of our failed finger-painter make it clear that she had no idea what was happening. After all, that finger paint looked like pudding!

Of course, these three children are not to blame. It's easy to remember that, for example, very few homes have finger paints available on a regular basis for preschooler use. So, instead of assuming that children have the understanding and skills to use classroom materials, we need to recognize children's need for instruction in using a classroom environment. And that means teaching things that, to adults, may seem obvious.

Instead of assuming children have the experience, knowledge, and skills to engage effectively in your classroom, consider each element of your design and ask: *How will I teach the use of this object or area?* Often, it's apparent that you need to take the time to explain; for example, it's easy to remember to teach the rules of a new board game you want to introduce. But *everything* requires this consideration, particularly more open-ended materials like blocks, crayons, and the like. They have a variety of uses and unclear rules.

It's your responsibility to make sure that all children have the opportunity to experience the things you have incorporated into your classroom environment. That requires multiple forms of instruction, not simply one-time, direct instruction using words—that just won't work for most preschoolers. Instead, you need to be ready to use multiple forms of instruction, including modeling, role-playing, and more. This is discussed in greater detail in chapter 4. Just like adults, children deserve dozens of opportunities to try and fail before they are expected to perform something with skill. So keep those other forms of instruction handy for the children struggling to learn.

## How Can I Make Sure Everyone Has Access to All Learning Experiences, Areas, and Materials?

One requirement of a quality preschool classroom is that every child has access to all of the learning experiences provided there. This requirement sounds simple enough at first. But thinking through questions of access will likely lead to some tricky challenges.

It's extremely satisfying to unpack new materials in a center while children are gathered around, shaking with anticipation. But that satisfaction can quickly turn to chaos if you haven't thought about some of the basic issues related to preschool crowds. How many children is too many children?

The answer to that question involves many different factors. One is square footage: how big is the area in which the group of children are located? A small area may only fit one or two children, meaning it presents access issues for any activities that aren't individual or paired. But even if you have a larger area, can you truly accommodate more children just because they can fit in the space? For example, do you have enough of the new materials for multiple children to use at the same time? And pay attention to what's popular: if there is only one T. rex in your 100-dinosaur package, you may be in trouble!

Finally, your access decisions need to account for children's developmental levels. To what extent are children playing independently or cooperatively? How skilled are your preschoolers at turn-taking and waiting? Are they getting into complicated arguments about who gets to do what? Since every area must support social and emotional development, you need to figure out the answers to these questions well before opening an area to children.

> One requirement of a quality preschool classroom is that every child has access to all of the learning experiences provided there. This requirement sounds simple enough at first. But thinking through questions of access will likely lead to some tricky challenges.

Different early childhood education approaches answer such questions differently. Some promote group self-regulation, expecting children to sort it out themselves. Others encourage collaborative, teacher-monitored systems that allow a certain number of children in an area. This treats the experience as an opportunity to scaffold executive function. Still others ask teachers to manage the situation entirely, leaving children out of the loop. Any of these theories might make sense in a given situation. It depends on the developmental levels of the children, your teacher-student ratio, and your developmental goals for the learning area.

There are simpler issues to take into account that still require some organizational time and effort. Most licensing and quality program standards require learning materials to be reachable by all children in your classroom, regardless of stature or ability. Storage containers need to be transparent whenever possible. Label them clearly with the languages of your classroom and photos of the objects, and place matching labels on the shelves that hold those containers. Remember, the whole classroom needs to be committed to supporting organization and availability: if you can't find it, it's not accessible!

Finally, recognize that a child's declaration of "Mine!" is developmentally appropriate behavior. This is particularly true for children new to classroom life. Learning how to take care of classroom items, to share, and to take turns are all key skills children need to learn in your classroom. Establish values-based ethics of care that you can state as community principles. Teach them proactively to help everyone build the community that serves everyone.

## Is This Stuff Fresh or Stale?

Once areas and materials are accessible, you need to continually evaluate whether they are being used. That means it's time to play a game that, in my house, we called "Yay or Nay."

Every change of seasons, the two adults and the two children in our household went through everything in their closets, in chests of drawers, under the beds, wherever clothes could be found. Everyone was expected to make a decision about whether something was still a "yay"—an appropriate garment that fit and looked good—or a "nay," something that no longer fit or wasn't going to be worn. Yays were returned to closets and chests of drawers, while nays were donated or, if in poor condition, tossed.

"Yay or Nay" translates very nicely into your preschool classroom! Simply pay attention over the course of a week to a given area or storage box. You will see whether children are still engaged by the center or set of materials, or whether it's time for a change. Often, the problem may not be the materials themselves but how you've used them. High-quality materials typically have multiple uses, in different situations and environments. A quick visit to the internet can reveal new, creative ways to redefine otherwise-tired materials. That said, the licensing or accreditation standards your program follows may require that materials be rotated after a certain number of weeks. Knowing what you have in storage for the next round is always a good idea.

**TO SPARK YOUR LEARNING...** Nadia Kenisha Bynoe and Angelique Thompson wrote an outstanding guide for applying child development principles to decision-making about materials and their use. Their book, *The Gift of Playful Learning* (2023), presents a powerful way to create material displays as "invitations" to children, activating their motivation to learn through playful problem-solving and collaboration.

## How Can I Cultivate and Promote an Ethic of Care for These Materials and Areas?

Keep in mind that every question about access is really a question of community. As children develop a theory of mind, empathy, and collaborative problem-solving skills, they themselves can take on much of the responsibility for guaranteeing equitable access in many areas of a classroom.

But to develop those skills, children need you to establish a clear sense of what exactly *community* means. Community relates to more than the interactions among humans. It also has to do with how those humans use and care for things and spaces in the community. Preschoolers learn from each other in ways that infants and toddlers cannot. And they establish and develop their sense of fairness and concern with adults like you as guides. This foundational social understanding can be the basis for developing a shared ethic of care for the classroom, learning areas, and materials.

Cultivating an ethic of care is very different from setting rules that children are expected to follow. Classroom rules routinely require authorities, usually teachers, to determine, legislate, and enforce them. Expecting children's compliance with these types of adult demands ignores children's rights and authority as creators of their own community. An ethic of care approaches these questions within a broad commitment to that community, one that grows from children's very own sense of justice and fairness.

Caring for each other shows up in ways that are probably familiar to you. For example, you have welcoming rituals and are sure to connect with each child every day. You support children who are having strong emotions or otherwise struggling, you go immediately to a child who has been hurt by another (instead of reprimanding the aggressor), and so on. You perform the ethic of care in every interaction with every child, because, as principle 2 reminds us, every interaction matters.

The same principle applies to things and the classroom environment as a whole. Caring for materials, areas, and the classroom community takes some responsive, creative thinking. Let's say that you are growing frustrated with the library area of your classroom. Children are leaving books on the floor, with their covers splayed open. Favorite books are showing their age, with torn pages here and there. Declaring that "we use gentle hands with books" clearly hasn't worked. That means it's time to perform the ethic of care in a creative, sustained way.

> Cultivating an ethic of care is very different from setting rules that children are expected to follow.

With a box, some tape, and some scissors, you can create a "book hospital," a place where the community takes care of injured books. Recruiting two or three children, you scour the room for injured books, picking them up gently and carrying them to the book hospital. Together, you diagnose the problem with each book. You come up with a treatment plan, doing all you can to repair the book. When you're done, you place the book back on the library shelf with a sense of gratitude and joy that you have demonstrated your ethic of care in this regard.

This approach requires you to determine what care looks like with each item in your room and in each area of your room. Children can help you with this task. At circle time, you can all work together to answer the question, "How do we take care of this?" Are there steps that the group can take to fix the problem? Are there certain tasks that require new classroom jobs or responsibilities?

And when something isn't receiving the level of care you feel it deserves, you can collaborate with children to identify the reasons for that lack of care. Be proactive, carefully avoiding blaming specific culprits. Focus instead on bringing more students into this community of care. By avoiding blame and activating shared responsibility, you communicate the ways in which your classroom is built on belonging, welcoming everyone.

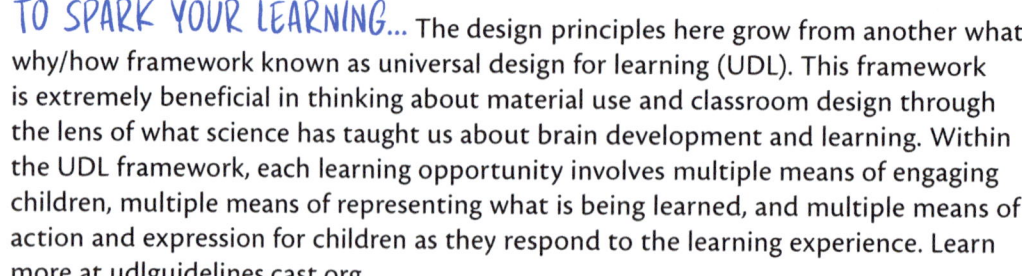

**TO SPARK YOUR LEARNING...** The design principles here grow from another what/why/how framework known as universal design for learning (UDL). This framework is extremely beneficial in thinking about material use and classroom design through the lens of what science has taught us about brain development and learning. Within the UDL framework, each learning opportunity involves multiple means of engaging children, multiple means of representing what is being learned, and multiple means of action and expression for children as they respond to the learning experience. Learn more at udlguidelines.cast.org.

# From Compliance to Ownership in Room Design

Another way to restate a commitment to a community ethic of care is to refer to principle 9. Instead of being rule-bound compliance enforcers, teachers become facilitators of children's ownership for the community in all its aspects. Activating children's ownership for everyone and everything in the community is a critical part of social development. And it makes for a much more enjoyable classroom for everyone involved.

Of course, this shift in attitude from compliance to ownership starts with you. When it comes to things like room design, developing a sense of ownership can feel frustrating when you just want to get through that licensing visit or accreditation review! As we discussed in chapter 2, this challenge will pop up in many different aspects of our work, given our extraordinary responsibility. Let's take a look at a set of issues that are part of any room design.

## Early Childhood Quality Standards

Virtually all early childhood classrooms are required to address a set of local, state, and national standards for quality. Districts and local early childhood organizations may have their own expectations for what should happen each day or week in your classroom. Those standards are likely to be informed by statewide expectations. These come from legislated statutes, quality rating and improvement systems, credential requirements, and other sources.

While those standards often differ significantly from state to state, many rely on a set of research-based standards and related tools found across the United States. For example, many organizations, districts, and states follow the early learning program standards created and maintained by the National Association for the Education of Young Children. These standards are used to determine NAEYC accreditation, which may be encouraged by your state's QRIS ratings. Similarly, many states use existing program or classroom assessments to determine quality, such as the Classroom Assessment Scoring System (CLASS®) and the Early Childhood Environment Rating Scale (ECERS®).

These assessments have become very powerful in the world of early childhood education. All are linked to requirements, quality ratings, and funding for programs. They're also linked to performance evaluation tools for specific classrooms or instructors. That high-stakes power can make them very scary indeed! So it's important to remember principle 9 and approach these standards by moving from compliance to ownership.

For example, the NAEYC standards are explicitly built to help teachers recognize what the research tells us about quality classrooms. The aim is to support ongoing quality improvement. And of course there's always something to improve! As one of my mentors likes to say, any program that gets a perfect rating is probably designing their program to get that high score, not for children. Instead, our goal is to find effective, responsive ways to support the learning and growth of the children in our care, using these standards as guides.

Approaching these standards with an opportunity mindset allows you to ask how children and families can benefit from them. Learning what ECERS might have to say about your library area, for example, could spark some ideas about how to make it more engaging. Reviewing NAEYC standards for outdoor play could help you rethink the constraints of your outdoor spaces. Embracing these standards with interest instead of anxiety is the best way to take advantage of the opportunities they offer.

TO SPARK YOUR LEARNING... NAEYC has devoted decades to exploring the research and best practices for early learning programs. Its accreditation system is the gold standard in many local and state systems. Read more about these standards at naeyc.org/our-work/families/10-naeyc-program-standards.

The Classroom Assessment Scoring System is used by many programs, states, and the Office of Head Start to measure classroom quality, focusing on interactions. Read more at eclkc.ohs.acf.hhs.gov/designation-renewal-system/article/use-classroom-assessment-scoring-system-class-head-start.

The Early Childhood Environment Rating Scale is also used extensively in early childhood systems; read more at ers.fpg.unc.edu/scales-early-childhood-environment-rating-scale-third-edition.

## Safety and Health Regulations

This book goes into great detail about most of the categories you'll find in early learning standards. However, there are other standards related to safety and health that require your careful attention to the very specific regulations in your own situation. Local and state fire codes; emergency preparedness routines; first aid and CPR training; cleaning, sanitizing, disinfecting, and handwashing expectations; regularly scheduled drills; food handling procedures—these are critical components of a wide range of programs, not just early childhood classrooms. They deserve your careful attention, so seek them out and master them!

There are also some safety and health regulations that are particular to the preschool children in your care. For example, all high-quality programs require active supervision of young children at all times. Both inside and outside the classroom, you'll want to monitor all children by sight and sound throughout the day. Make sure all teachers are able to take positions within the room that promote careful supervision. Often that means sharing the responsibility to monitor individuals or small groups, as well as more challenging large groups. Let's face it: no one wants to work with a teacher who sits with the same two children all day long, especially if they have their back to the rest of the room!

**TO SPARK YOUR LEARNING...** The Office of Head Start has an excellent guide documenting the nuances of active supervision. You can find it at eclkc.ohs.acf.hhs.gov/safety-practices/article/active-supervision. Why not download this tool and review it on your own or with your team?

A well-designed classroom will take these regulations into account. For example, you are far less likely to require your first aid kit if you've thought carefully about traffic patterns for your endlessly active students. How do they enter the classroom? How do they exit the classroom? How can they flow through the classroom? And you cannot assume orderly lines with children waiting patiently! Remember that they are all developing key gross motor skills, impulse control, and the ability to perceive other humans like themselves. Those developmental demands may make for lots of traffic jams in a poorly designed classroom.

Similarly, you'll want to think carefully about where you position yourself within the room throughout the day. This is not only a central question for monitoring children's behavior and interacting with them in productive ways. It's also a question of your own physical health. Positioning adult furniture in appropriate places can help limit the ergonomic challenges all early childhood educators face. Think about how often you walk, sit, kneel, and bend over throughout the day. Your safety and health matter too!

## "That's Not Safe!"

The previous two sections refer to state, federal, and national organization standards. But we can't move on from discussions of compliance without talking about one particular teacher perspective with which you may already be familiar.

As we know, preschoolers learn by making mistakes, bumping into other children, falling off of playground components, and regularly taking risks that weren't very well thought out in the first place. And in many preschool classrooms, there is often at least one risk-averse adult who is easy to identify. Just listen for the person who repeatedly declares, "That's not safe!"

The high activity level of preschoolers means that bumps, scrapes, bruises, and cuts are the norm. It's understandable that preschool teachers would like to eliminate these sorts of concerns. This is especially true if an adult family member is concerned about a child's safety. However, these situations require reconsideration and reflection. Here's an example from my own experience.

When I was a preschool director in Rhode Island, I found myself in a sticky situation involving some old, expensive playground equipment. It frustrated me to no end. The equipment was designed to incorporate risks that were appropriate when the equipment was installed. But it was no longer approved by the playground safety authorities we trusted. However, we couldn't just fix the problem. Making any modifications to these expensive pieces of equipment would immediately void their warranty and make us liable for any injuries that occurred. It was a real conundrum!

To get unstuck, we started talking as a community about the difference between *hazard* and *risk*. Hazard means that something is predisposed to be dangerous. All hazards must be removed from all classrooms, as the previous section discussed in detail.

But risk is an inherent element of children's learning, starting at a very early age and continuing throughout the preschool years (and later in life!). Indeed, many foundational child development studies are predicated on the question of how a child determines risk and acts as a result. In the "visual cliff" experiment, for example, an infant crawls up to the edge of a horizontal plexiglass window. They must measure the risk of continuing across the fake precipice against a parent's encouragement. (To see this in action, go to YouTube and search "visual cliff experiment.") Risks produce opportunities for motor, social, emotional, and cognitive development throughout the day. Risks develop pride when they pay off and promote resilience and perseverance when they do not.

> Risks produce opportunities for motor, social, emotional, and cognitive development throughout the day. Risks develop pride when they pay off and promote resilience and perseverance when they do not.

These insights became the lens through which I watched the children and faculty on the playground, and I discovered some interesting trends. I tallied the number of times teachers interacted with children in a mode of compliance. I found that over half of the things that they said referenced hazards that didn't exist. Children climbing up a slide were told that they needed to get down or they might "break their necks." Other children were told that they were "running too fast."

Meanwhile, the teachers really didn't like being on the playground—which made a lot of sense! They felt like they were security cameras, not teachers. They were on edge all the time trying to "keep children safe." They weren't doing anything wrong or harmful. They simply were unaware that they had closed down nearly every opportunity for children to take risks.

So I decided it was time for *me* to take a risk. Over the weekend, I worked with a construction crew to demolish and remove that hazardous structure. While we were at it, we cleared out some other items that were prompting the most worrisome compliance speech from teachers. And when my faculty came to work on Monday morning, they were aghast. Suddenly, our playground looked empty to them, bereft of any interesting activities for children. They didn't like it, or me, one bit.

As they went out on the playground over the next few days, I reminded them of the hazard/risk difference. I encouraged them to shift from monitoring safety compliance to encouraging children's autonomy. We reviewed certain areas and discussed the various risks. We came up with descriptive language for children to consider. Together, we wrote new sentences to emphasize children's ownership and autonomy, such as "You are in charge of your body" and "I wonder what would happen if you took that risk?"

Not quite convinced, the teachers took a deep breath and gave it a try. The transformation was rapid and astonishing to us all. Children suddenly were running across the playground, climbing on logs, jumping and rolling and bumping into each other. Meanwhile, teachers helped them make decisions about all of these different activities with questions, encouragement, and general support. When risky behavior produced proud success, teachers celebrated with children. When risky behavior led to a stumble, teachers supported the stumbler and encouraged another try or a revised approach. Facilitating children's consideration of risk became the norm. And the compliance demands disappeared forever.

The faculty was relieved. Instead of worrying about safety, they were helping children think about risks themselves, and they were focused on their roles as educators. To be sure, we got rid of hazardous equipment. But the major transformation was a mindset shift: we reframed our understanding of hazard versus risk. This shift allowed the teachers to reconnect to why they joined the profession in the first place.

# Classroom Geography

Let's now take a look at the different physical aspects of your classroom one at a time.

## Doors and Entryways

The entrance into your classroom is one of the first things children and parents will see. As a result, many teachers cover their doors and the areas nearby with all sorts of paper. We post newsletters, calendars, menus, children's artwork, forms that need filling out, photographs . . . it's a long list! And let's face it: how often do you stop by the bulletin board at the grocery store and read each one of the items posted there?

If your school asks parents to walk their children into and out of the classroom, be sure to consider the reality of arrival and departure. Few parents are likely to have lots of time to linger by your door. They prefer to focus on their child (and probably their lives outside the school walls). That means that doors and entryways are rarely the best places to communicate important information. In addition, you want to do all you can to avoid creating excess traffic when lots of people are entering and exiting the room!

If you do choose to post items on or around your door, keep those transition-related challenges in mind. For children, the transition into the classroom often requires significant effort. Consider activities that can spark learning at arrival, such as having students sign in for the day at a table in the hallway. Be sure to keep the sight lines clear both inside and outside the room. Remove any obstacles that block vision or accessibility.

Finally, pay close attention to the children who find the transition into your classroom emotionally challenging. What can you do to promote their sense of belonging? Of course, every adult in the room should greet every child and family member by name as they transition into the classroom. Those greetings are essential for children's well-being. And parents, siblings, and other family members want to feel that they belong too!

Consider designing a multistep routine for children and family members to follow at arrival. Plan simple, sequenced tasks that children can repeat and master with the help of their adult partners. For example, place a laminated sign-in sheet outside the door on a low desk, with large blank spaces below each child's first name. This can both activate a required fine motor activity and help a family member assess their child's progress with that critical task.

# Surfaces

As a school director I routinely asked my teachers to distinguish between two types of stuff that goes on walls, windows, and other surfaces: Does this item promote learning and community, or is it just decor? This question is the key to determining how to approach surfaces.

Let's revisit the example of purchased alphabets. Classrooms often have several on display, placed high on the wall, far above where children can easily use them as a resource. Unless you're referring to those alphabets routinely throughout the day, they're just clutter.

We know that most children learn about letters starting with the first letter in their first name. Supporting children's understanding of the alphabet, as a result, might change over time. At the start of the year, you could create an alphabet with just letters of all children's first names, leaving spaces for the other letters to be added later. Each of the first set of letters could be accompanied by a photograph of the child or children whose names start with it. This personalized alphabet would be great to use during circle time at the start of the day. You could point at each letter and photo as you greet each child. That means the alphabet needs to be low on the wall, where you and the children can use it.

As the year unfolds, and children start identifying other letters, you can add those letters with pictures of people and objects that correspond to them. As children develop the ability to write letters, you can add their own handwritten versions. In different areas of the classroom, you could create similar alphabets for important vocabulary related to that area. This would allow you to refer to those words and concepts during learning activities.

> Document and celebrate children's learning by displaying their writing, their artworks, photographs of learning activities, and more. Label these displays with descriptions of the developmental concepts being depicted.

Remember that alphabets are only one form of environmental print that you and the children can use throughout the day. Label everything you can label. Use not only English but also any other languages your classroom's families use, and add photos of the labeled items. Display a visual daily schedule, with words and photos of children performing each activity. This will help you support children who struggle with transitions. Similarly, a job chart designed so that children can attach their names and photos to a given task can be used by everyone throughout the day.

Of course, displays can also help you build community. For example, in your block area you could display photographs of buildings, parks, and roads nearby, referencing them with children as they play. Document and celebrate children's learning by displaying their writing, their artworks, photographs of learning activities, and more. Label these displays with descriptions of the developmental concepts being depicted.

Many classrooms also have an area dedicated to displaying children's family members, with names and photos of important people placed at children's height. When building such a display, keep in mind principle 5. Design your display so that every child and family is included. For families going through various transitions, these displays can be very complicated. You'll need to be sensitive to every family's structure and desires.

Finally, as you design your displays, be sure to consider confidentiality. Children in the child welfare system may have restrictions for photographs. All information related to a medical or developmental concern (allergies, for example) is inappropriate to display. Be sure that you understand your local and state requirements for such information. Work with your administrators to determine appropriate ways to keep important information readily available but for your eyes only.

## Outdoors

Unlike indoor spaces, it's rare that teachers have much design input into the outdoor spaces that they have available. So instead of an extensive description of how to build an outdoor learning space, here are a few basic tips.

First, remember that going outdoors is not recess! Everywhere children go is an environment that can support their learning and growth, and the outdoors is no exception. As a result, time spent outdoors requires thoughtful planning, instruction, and materials. Remember to think of the outdoors as providing an opportunity for learning with unique qualities you cannot replicate inside.

Take, for example, open space. It's no accident that many preschoolers immediately burst into a full dash as soon as they get outside. The outdoors is a great place for developing gross motor skills. Large, open spaces that allow for running and chasing provide opportunities that are literally unavailable inside. For boisterous preschoolers enclosed in your classroom, outdoor running and chasing is likely a relief!

Similarly, the outdoors is a naturally changing environment. Temperature, moisture, animals, and plants all characterize this fascinating space. As such, the outdoors offers a unique opportunity for exploration and wonder, no matter the weather. With effective, engaging prompts you provide, children can be researchers investigating flora and fauna. You can create experiments related to environmental conditions and the like.

One final note. Most early childhood quality standards insist that outdoor activity should be a priority regardless of the weather unless it is unsafe. You will likely encounter colleagues and family members who disagree! So it's important that you help family members understand the *why* for outdoor learning. Emphasize the learning experiences that happen there, with detailed documentation.

As you do, keep your equity lens handy and make sure you are taking into account the different cultural norms concerning warmth, cold, dirt, and water. Start conversations with parents early, before you are forced to have them. A frustrated parent may not understand why their child is outside when it's snowing or why there are grass stains on those new pants!

TO SPARK YOUR LEARNING... A classic book that belongs on every early childhood professional's shelf is *Lens on Outdoor Learning* by Wendy Banning and Ginny Sullivan (2010). They do a fantastic job of linking early learning standards to dozens of engaging experiences for children in natural environments. You'll generate endless opportunities for children's learning with their guidance.

The entire classroom environment is both your responsibility and your teaching partner's, and it's a big one! Well-designed, developmentally appropriate learning spaces support children's growth in many ways. They help children engage in self-initiated play, encourage them to maintain an ethic of care, and make their learning more exciting. What's more, engaged children who care about their environment create fewer unpleasant chores for you, allowing you greater focus on that learning.

Of course, designing a learning environment from top to bottom can feel like a daunting task! The planning activities from chapter 2 can help. First, determine those things in your control that you can change and those that you can't. Then, identify the issues that are most important and urgent, in order to tackle those first. Considering the results of that work as you review this chapter will help you develop a rough plan for prioritizing your room design and materials-planning efforts.

Finally, just like the children in your care, the room environment will change over time. Children's bodies and interests will shift the way they interact with different areas. Items that are compelling learning materials one week can be boring the next. And in many classrooms, children come and go over the course of the year. So keep this chapter handy! It will help you adjust your classroom environment when your observations of the space suggest it's time for some changes.

# Your Story as a Professional Educator and Caregiver

Review the topics covered in this chapter. Then grab your journal or a piece of paper and write your answers to these four reflection questions:

1. Walk through your classroom, identifying the basic built features (doors, windows, sinks, floor types, and so on). Which of these things are the key elements to take into account as you make your design decisions?

2. What expertise, knowledge, and insight about each learning area or material can you design into the classroom right now?

3. As you review the chapter, what do you think you need to learn more about to help you serve children better?

4. What learning story do you want to tell about yourself on your journey to become the best educator and caregiver you can be?

CHAPTER 4

# The Curriculum, Instruction, and Assessment Cycle

You've filled your classroom with all sorts of interesting, engaging materials. You've thought through how the space should be arranged. Now it's time to spark the learning! The cycle that we use in early childhood education for making decisions and enacting them has three components.

*Curriculum* is a written plan for everything that happens in your classroom. Curriculum includes learning goals related to both content and skills, planned activities to promote goals for all children, daily schedules and regular routines, and so on (NAEYC, n.d.). It also includes learning plans your team develops, published curriculum products, supplemental curriculum materials, weekly lesson plans, and more. If it's a written description of what you should do in your classroom, it's part of your overall curriculum package.

*Instruction* refers to all the actions you take in promoting children's learning and growth. In early childhood education, we stress the importance of intentional instruction. This means reflecting on yourself and the children you teach, your curriculum goals, and the best instructional strategies you can use in a given situation. While it is important to bring intentionality to everything you do, it's just as important to recognize that your unintentional actions instruct young children. So part of intentional instruction is noticing what sorts of unintentional instruction you are providing!

*Assessment* is both the formal and informal use of your knowledge of child development to develop understanding of children's learning and growth. We now have a wide variety of assessment tools available to choose from that cover all levels and areas of children's development. We use these tools in an ongoing manner to adjust our teaching, referred to as *formative assessment*. And we use them at the end of longer learning cycles such as quarters or years to assess our efforts over time. This is referred to as *summative assessment*. Skillful early childhood educators are constantly performing informal assessments. We are always observing our students objectively and nonjudgmentally with a commitment to seeing the whole child.

**TO SPARK YOUR LEARNING...** NAEYC has family-friendly language that you can use to help others understand these abstract concepts. Visit naeyc.org/our-work/families/10-naeyc-program-standards. In addition, many states, federal programs, and curriculum and assessment systems have their own helpful explanations of this cycle.

# Engaging the Curriculum/Instruction/ Assessment Cycle

Far from being boring paperwork and mindless teaching, this cycle becomes the energy you feed into the classroom to make it go. In the best classrooms, curriculum, instruction, and assessment are the musical instruments that are constantly playing in the background. The result is that everyone—children, teachers, administrators, and family members—is dancing to the same symphony. And you are the conductor!

Of course, in a world with dozens of curriculum options, assessment tools, and instructional methods, it's impossible for me to know exactly what sheet music you are using! So in order to help you get ready to perform that music with the appropriate mindset, let's review our ten principles. Each one relates to the three elements of this cycle.

## 1. Remember: Education Is Care, and Care Is Education

In early childhood education, curriculum focuses on content that emphasizes basic human traits. We plan supports for self-care life skills like tying your shoes and waiting. We create opportunities for children to recognize both who they are and who others are as well. And we help them care for themselves and others. We provide caring support for children because we recognize these goals require real effort from each child. Skills that may seem obvious to adults take persistence and resilience for children to learn.

The curriculum, assessment, and instruction cycle is built on the recognition that education and care go hand in hand. Every component of curriculum, from letter recognition to color recognition to developing executive function skills, unfolds within instruction built on the caring relationships in your classroom. As a result, curriculum planning requires you to foster positive relationships, not only with each of the children, but also among them as a group.

Similarly, assessment must take into account the relationships teachers have with their students. Unfortunately, not every assessment method is designed to do that. I've seen teachers perform large group assessments where children, one at a time, go up to the whiteboard to be assessed for letter recognition. This creates a challenging environment that puts the assessments of individual children on public display. It also forces every student to wait for nearly twenty minutes as the method unfolds. The method may harvest required assessment data, but it places an unfair expectation on young children (as it would on anyone, for that matter)!

This is why it's important to attend to children's experiences when you administer assessments. In addition, you should regularly assess your room's health as a community. That means taking time to pay attention to children's belonging, the quality of basic social interactions, and each child's emotional regulation. You don't need a formal assessment tool to care for children in this way!

One last note on this principle. Equating education and care means that, in everything we do, we value what others sometimes call "soft skills." I've never liked that term,

> Children's academic success throughout their schooling requires sophisticated executive functioning skills, emotional regulation, and the ability to read complex social expectations.

as it suggests that education is the real goal and care is secondary. Yet the neurological research points to a very clear conclusion. Children's academic success throughout their schooling requires sophisticated executive functioning skills, emotional regulation, and the ability to read complex social expectations. These skills are built moment by moment in early childhood classrooms that prioritize these seemingly "soft" elements.

So in early childhood education we recognize that there's nothing "soft" about these skills at all. They require truly hard work both from children and from you! And, without this foundation, no later academic growth can occur. A quality early childhood classroom recognizes this in every element of its curriculum, assessment, and instruction.

## 2. Make Every Interaction Matter (Because Every Interaction Matters)

At first, it may seem that this principle only applies to instruction. After all, the teaching interactions you have with children comprise the bulk of your day. In that regard, curriculum is a container for meaningful interactions between you and your students.

But this principle applies to more than your instructional interactions with children. For example, we want every interaction between children and curricular content to matter as well. That's why good early childhood teachers are always careful when using a preset, theme-based curriculum that dictates specific content. To be sure, a deep dive into something compelling is a hallmark of any good curriculum. It allows for broad vocabulary development, deeper critical thinking skills, and project-based excursions into rich content. But a good teacher is always paying close attention to whether children are truly engaged or not!

Put differently, if the content doesn't engage children and inspire them to learn, it doesn't really matter to their learning. As a result, make sure to identify content that children can interact with in ways that matter to them. One simple way to do this is to listen carefully to what sparks interest in children. Thankfully, young children are very good at telling us what matters to them! So finding ways to incorporate their specific and varied interests in your classroom is not only beneficial for children's learning. Doing so will also create far more enjoyable classroom experiences for you as an educator.

Finally, as discussed above, recognize that assessments can often be unpleasant experiences for children. This is especially true if the assessment frustrates the child in any way. Some formal assessments do not take the child's experience into account. As you administer assessments, always prioritize your interaction with the child throughout the experience. Make the interaction matter.

## 3. Prioritize Honesty, Transparency, and Trust with Everyone

There are many ways this principle applies to curriculum, assessment, and instruction.

Let's take a curriculum goal such as turn-taking. What would it mean to prioritize honesty, transparency, and trust with everyone regarding that goal? For starters, every member of your teaching team would agree that the goal should be a priority for all interactions with children and each other. That means that adults, not just children, honestly reflect on their turn-taking, communicating with each other when it's going well and when it isn't. In addition, if a member of your team has concerns about the goal or the instructional strategies you'll use, they would trust the team enough to be honest about that concern. This litmus test of honesty, transparency, and trust helps your team collaborate more effectively throughout the day.

Of course, you would want to keep family members in the loop about the week's curriculum goals and how you will assess whether children are meeting those goals. You could also share with families the instructional practices you're using to address goals. This promotes transparency and offers them strategies they can use at home.

Just as importantly, sharing curriculum goals with the children themselves is absolutely critical! Help them understand why you're working on a topic and discuss what you hope they'll be able to do as they meet that goal. These simple acts of transparency will cultivate trust with children. It will also help them develop the self-awareness and metacognition they need.

Finally, it is essential to approach all forms of assessment with a clear-eyed commitment to honesty and transparency. Formal assessment tools are essential to determining quality in early childhood programs. Only a few decades ago, we had few, if any, valid and reliable assessment tools. Each program had to build its own. But now there are many, and they are built into well-established requirements from districts, states, accreditation agencies, and others. These research-based tools are a fact of our profession, and very important elements of our work.

But let's be honest and transparent. When used inappropriately, these tools can create anxiety and frustration for educators, children, and families. That is often the case when we forget what a given assessment tool was designed to do. Like any tool, it has a specific, limited purpose. That means that there are many other ways it can be

> As an early childhood professional, it's critical that you are keenly aware of the purpose of a given assessment tool. Keep an eye out for inappropriate use.

used that ignore that purpose. You wouldn't use a screwdriver to hammer in a nail, but unfortunately people often use assessments for purposes that are different from what's intended.

As an early childhood professional, it's critical that you are keenly aware of the purpose of a given assessment tool. Keep an eye out for inappropriate use. Conversations about assessments and their appropriate use are particularly important to have with colleagues and family members. If you think that a tool is being used inappropriately, it's time for honesty and transparency with your administrator. Using assessments in honest and transparent ways creates opportunities for building, and not harming, trust.

## 4. Keep Your Equity Lens Handy

Of course, prioritizing honesty, transparency, and trust is central to using your equity lens. Recognizing and honoring the diversity of each child, adult, family, and community in your classroom must be built into the structure of your curriculum. At times, you may find that some curricular content doesn't fully address the realities and experiences of those you serve. In those situations, being equitable means acknowledging and addressing the inequalities embedded in that content. Then you take steps to build curriculum that is truly inclusive for your particular classroom.

Let's take a simple example regarding book selection. Every children's book refers to a world of experience that assumes some prior knowledge. A book about cows that can type, for example, requires some recognition of farms and rural life. Any of these elements could be mysterious to some or all young children. That mystery would block their comprehension and confuse them.

Children expand their learning in the dynamic space between their prior knowledge and skills and the new knowledge and skills that they will gain. A book about life on a farm can activate a child's existing knowledge of farms, cows, and writing as it expands their knowledge of those twentieth-century machines called typewriters. So the content you provide should activate that prior knowledge and build on it with new information.

Be on the lookout for any biases built into the content you use. This is particularly true for any content that suggests that there are universal norms related to human existence. For example, quality books acknowledge a wide range of diversity regarding children's body types, skin colors, and hair types. Meanwhile, there are others that do not reflect that diversity and may suggest that certain body types are norms. Suggestions of norms are very harmful for children who can't see their bodies or skin or hair in the content your curriculum is promoting. They are also harmful for the children who see only themselves and assume they are better because they are "the norm." So make sure you have a wide variety of curricular content reflecting all sorts of humans. A variety of family arrangements, languages, neighborhoods, foods, and so on is essential.

**TO SPARK YOUR LEARNING...** Looking for some useful lists of books that relate to human diversity? The good folks at We Need Diverse Books have done your homework for you! Check out diversebooks.org for dozens of useful links to lists across many different topics.

In addition, turn your equity lens toward your assessment practices. It's not easy to identify biases that are baked into certain contemporary research-based assessments. Instead, focus your attention on the fact that a tool is only as effective as its user, and we all carry our own biases. As a result, you need to acknowledge that even relatively equitable assessments can be used to inequitable ends.

We know, for example, that children of color, especially boys, are expelled from preschool for behavioral reasons at alarming rates (Novak 2023). This overrepresentation suggests that the responsible educators weren't able to recognize the personal assumptions they held regarding children's behavior and cultural bias. Whether they used formal or informal assessment tools to make these decisions didn't matter. As discussed above, inequity can mean that the children who most need our support in early childhood classrooms are the very ones prevented from receiving that support. So we need to keep a close eye on how we use these powerful assessment tools.

## 5. Design and Plan for Every Child and Family

Principle 4 leads directly into principle 5. A powerful equity lens is critical as you determine the instructional strategies that you will use for the different children and families you serve. A key component of instruction involves making adjustments for the needs of children. We adjust for them individually and in aggregate. We meet children where they are, and not the other way around.

Here's a simple tool that you can use every week to make sure you're designing and planning for every child in your classroom. Create a "meaningful interaction" checklist. Make multiple copies (or a laminated sheet) of the full list of children in your class. At the beginning of each week, use a new list. Keep the list and a pen or pencil handy throughout the day. Every time you have a meaningful interaction for a minute or two with a child, put a check next to their name on your list. Then, at the end of each week, take a close look at your list.

At first, you may think the list is about the children in your class. After all, that's their names on the list! But this list is actually about you—if you can perceive it through your equity lens.

The children with lots of checks next to their names say something about the types of children to whom you are drawn. Those children are likely receiving a large amount of supportive instructional guidance from you. They also are receiving caring attachment experiences throughout the day. It's likely that they are the children you imagine when you are designing your lesson plans. Children with few or no check marks are not receiving that same level of instructional support. And they aren't likely to be the ones you think of when you're planning.

> A key component of instruction involves making adjustments for the needs of children. We adjust for them individually and in aggregate. We meet children where they are, and not the other way around.

Each week, this exercise gives you an opportunity to confront your own behaviors. It allows you to make adjustments to create a more equitable classroom. There's no human on the planet who would distribute their check marks perfectly equally every week! So cut yourself some slack. Week to week, make adjustments to prioritize the children you've inadvertently neglected. Meanwhile, take a few moments to reflect on why you seem to avoid certain children while being drawn to others. There's always something in those check marks for you to explore.

A parallel process is useful for making sure your curriculum is reaching every child. You can use the same list of children to track their engagement in different activities, learning centers, and other elements of your curriculum. A child who gets few check marks in this exercise is likely to be disengaged in your classroom. That disengagement, built by repeated unsuccessful experiences, can cultivate a deep-seated belief that school is not for them.

That's precisely when you want to rethink your curriculum design, prioritizing the children who would most benefit from some changes. What content gets them excited? What sorts of activities help them engage? And this is a good time for partnerships with family members. Those are good questions to ask—and they'll likely have interesting answers!

# 6. Do Your Best with What You've Got

It's happened to all of us. A new expectation or demand comes down the road, requiring us to try out something we've never seen before. Change is always difficult. Getting to know a new curriculum, assessment tool, or instructional approach can be a real challenge and at times feels overwhelming.

But this relentless change is one of the conditions of our field at the moment. We are taking more thoughtful looks at what we do and how we do it. We are identifying areas for improvement and enacting those improvements. It's actually a sign of growth within our profession, though a tricky one to handle at times.

In the midst of all this change, we tend to react in two ways. For some of us, it's very easy to become self-critical. We get anxious about some skill we are lacking or understanding we haven't mastered in order to make this new thing work. That's the way I am at first: my inner critic immediately starts telling me that I should have known this already or mastered this skill long ago.

For those of us who don't default to self-blame, we can always blame the thing itself! Indeed, I've heard many complaints about excellent assessment tools that don't do something someone wants. It's something it was never designed to do in the first place! But that doesn't stop some educators from complaining that they can't drill a hole with a wrench.

Enacting this principle to do the best with what you've got means establishing two solid mindsets regarding the curriculum, assessment, and instruction cycle. The first mindset is recognizing that you simply can't do everything perfectly. That means accepting the anxiety that comes with trying new things. Approach the gaps you discover with a commitment to a growth mindset. How might you approach math differently in this lesson, setting aside your own long-standing math anxiety, for example? What is this mysterious aspect of child development you have to track on a new assessment tool? What additional perspectives does it offer on the children you serve?

This approach is especially important and powerful when it comes to instructional strategies. Having your teaching methods critiqued is difficult, and it's easy to take those critiques personally. But one of the ways a coach can support you is by noticing things you could do more effectively. It's not because they want to shame you. It's because there's a gap in your instructional tool kit you need to fill so your students can thrive and you can be more effective.

But sometimes, in our own self-critical brains, it's hard to separate the ways we go about teaching from the people that we are. We all have our go-to instructional approaches, the things that we learned and found effective early on. (These probably corresponded to how we function in the world in general.) Some teachers love to sit on the floor and play along with small groups of children in learning centers. They rarely choose direct instruction to a large group unless forced to do so. Other teachers think direct instruction at circle time is always the way to go, the only "real teaching." They seem never to be on the floor playing with the kids. For both types of teachers, the instructional strategy simply reflects who they are.

As a result, trying out a new instructional strategy often feels disorienting. It's like learning a new language. Developing comfort in a new approach takes time and effort—it won't feel like "who you are" for a good long while! That's why perseverance is so important. If you've discovered a gap in your instructional tool kit, that means that there are some children you aren't reaching as effectively as you could (and you probably know it). So to do the best with what you've got, you need to encourage yourself to move past self-blame and discomfort and into perseverance and growth.

> Developing comfort in a new approach takes time and effort—it won't feel like "who you are" for a good long while! That's why perseverance is so important.

Meanwhile, recognize that the annoying curriculum, inadequate assessment, or awkward instructional approach was created by other imperfect humans! Just like you, those humans did the best with what they had. So, along with a mindset that accepts imperfections, you need to activate an opportunity mindset. How can imperfect you take advantage of imperfect tools to improve what you do?

Principle 6 reminds you that, whenever possible, it's best to set your ego and its criticisms aside. Recognize that there is no curriculum on the planet that will perfectly correspond with your desires. Every assessment tool has annoying limitations that you will discover in using it. Most new instructional approaches feel weird when you first use them, and they may feel weird for a long time. It doesn't seem that way at first, but curriculum, assessment, and instructional strategies are thoroughly human, and thus imperfect, products.

You can approach these imperfections by leaning into a concept discussed in chapter 2, your professional use of self. You can activate both yourself and your curricula as resources. Do this by engaging your own identity, experience, and expertise in a professional manner that's aligned with your principles. The easiest way to lean into your professional use of self is, of course, by putting children at the center of your reflections. When you feel criticism rising up, recognize that criticism for what it is. It's both an easy way out and a disservice to the children you serve. Instead, realign your mindset and look for the opportunities that these components provide for the children in your classroom. You'll be glad you did!

## 7. Celebrate Successes and Rethink Flops

The quality of both your curriculum and your instruction can be wildly improved by reflecting on this important principle, and it's the central purpose of all assessment. What's working? What's not? What does that mean?

There is no question that, throughout your classroom, you will regularly experience moments of great engagement: a lesson you designed with thoughtful instructional components provides lots of opportunities for many children in your classroom. And of course, sometimes the decisions you make will flop: a lesson you thought would be a hit gets little interest from children. Or an instructional choice you make turns out to drive children away from learning instead of toward it.

Engaging this principle will bring you back to the foundations of problem-solving from chapter 2. First, establish a reflective mindset—the attitude that the situation presents a rich teaching moment. This is important whether the situation is positive or negative. What exactly happened? Who was involved? Has it happened before? And, most importantly, why did it happen?

Once again, you'll need to remember that asking *why* should prompt a discussion about contributing factors. What specific elements contributed to the success or flop? It's easy to do when things go well. But you may need to remind yourself, your team, and the children to avoid blame when exploring the factors that led to a flop.

Finally, pay close attention to the first word in the principle. Take the time to celebrate when things go well. Some of us have developed a complicated relationship to celebrating successes. We are more likely to downplay a positive experience or even treat it as not particularly meaningful. But both the adults and the children in preschool classrooms benefit from the energy generated by legitimate, authentic positive experiences. Let's take advantage when life presents us with things to celebrate!

## 8. Lead with Collaboration and Communication

We've discussed the importance of honest and transparent communication, the key foundations for building trust. So to activate principle 8, let's engage a simple strategy: state the obvious.

Teachers' spoken communication often leaps over content that they think doesn't need to be said out loud. For example, you set up a learning activity in the math center and begin scaffolding children's engagement. In any moment of the interaction, what you're trying to accomplish with a particular child may seem understandable to you. After all, you know what methods you're using, what goals you have for the children, and so on. But it's entirely possible that other folks, children and adults both, may not understand what you do in that moment.

So it's almost always a really good idea for you to state the obvious. This is particularly true with young children, for whom "obvious" concepts may be truly confusing. Young children work hard to learn concepts that most adults take for granted. For example, children may not understand cause and effect, the notion of time, and the fact that other people exist and have minds like their own.

Of course, something that's obvious to one adult may be new information to another! So it's also beneficial for adults to declare to their colleagues things they think are obvious. Even if the information isn't new to someone else, saying it out loud activates their prior knowledge. This helps get you both on the same page. An act that seems perfectly straightforward to you likely involves multiple steps and a variety of interrelated concepts. These are all excellent things to say out loud.

Let's take developmentally appropriate practice as an example. In order to understand and enact DAP, an educator needs to:

**a.** have a comprehensive understanding of child development across several domains;

**b.** be able to observe a child in an objective manner, keeping their own biases in check;

**c.** assess the child's knowledge and skills across those developmental domains based on the observed behavior or performance;

**d.** review a wide array of instructional practices and select the most appropriate one; and

**e.** perform that instructional practice to support the child's development in those domains.

Can you see why early childhood education is one of the most demanding professions on the planet? There's a lot going on there! Communicating each of those steps helps others understand the different components of the curriculum, assessment, and instruction cycle.

In this way, effective communication promotes collaboration throughout the cycle. There may be a hierarchy on your team in terms of position and training, with a lead teacher holding certain responsibilities and an assistant teacher holding others. But true collaboration is required to implement curriculum well, make thoughtful assessments, and provide effective instruction. There may be differences of responsibility for various components among your team, to be sure. But you support children's learning and growth when all the adults in the classroom are on the same page.

## 9. Move from Compliance to Ownership

Principle 9 is important throughout every aspect of your professional life. But it's hard to imagine any aspect where it is more meaningful than within the curriculum, assessment, and instruction cycle.

For starters, operating in compliance mode within this cycle is harmful to children: Designing a curricular unit using a cut-and-paste lesson plan you randomly pulled from social media. Rushing through a mandatory assessment. Sleepwalking through a required literacy activity. You get the picture—and it's not a pretty one for you or the children.

And let's face it: we've all been that colleague at one point or another for at least a moment or two. It's not fun. Being a teacher who approaches curriculum, assessment, and instruction as compliance-based activities is first and foremost unpleasant for that very teacher.

I believe strongly that everybody who goes into education, especially early childhood education, cares about kids. People may care differently, and they may care about different things. But the faculty I've met over the decades are deeply committed to supporting children's learning and growth. However, a mix of challenges can lead teachers to feeling bitter and burned out. We work in a profession that doesn't compensate people fairly, struggles to staff classrooms fully, and expects us to perform transformative miracles with struggling children and families.

Ownership is an antidote to that bitter burnout. Taking ownership helps ensure engagement with the curriculum, instruction, and assessment. It will lead to a more rewarding day for you and the children than moving through the day with a mindset of compliance. And finding ways to connect to children by activating their learning and growth—isn't that why you chose to work in education in the first place?

Let's take an example that can be frustrating for early childhood educators: kindergarten readiness. There are historical tensions between the play-based, developmentally appropriate practices in the early childhood profession and the curricular and instructional expectations in K–12 educational settings. Instructional practices that emphasize play for four- and five-year-olds may frustrate teachers who have found direct instruction beneficial for their students. And powerful assessments, especially related to literacy, may create anxiety as you try to embrace the research about what's right for children at this age.

Approaching these issues from a perspective of ownership may require you to do a little bit of extra work, but it's worth it. Instead of complying with the kindergarten readiness expectations handed to you, why not deepen your understanding by spending time in an actual kindergarten classroom? Even better, is it possible for you to visit one with some of your students, so that all of you can get a sense of what it's like? In addition, buy your kindergarten teacher colleague a cup of coffee after work one day and ask her what she hopes for from her students. It may be the best five dollars you ever spend!

> Taking ownership helps ensure engagement with the curriculum, instruction, and assessment. It will lead to a more rewarding day for you and the children than moving through the day with a mindset of compliance.

A deeper understanding of kindergarten readiness as teachers and children experience it in real kindergarten classrooms helps you move from compliance to ownership. And in my experience, it's a big relief. What you're likely to discover is that kindergarten teachers want children who want to engage with school. They want children who know how to be successful and who have developed good strategies for collaborating with others. Knowing this will help you own your classroom's curriculum, assessment, and instructional cycle with an eye toward the expectations that will help children thrive. It's a much more enjoyable way for you to tackle kindergarten readiness, don't you think?

Owning all the components of the cycle is not only a way of serving other people in your classroom. It's a way of serving your best self.

## 10. When in Doubt, Take a Look from a Child's Perspective

One of the most rewarding ways to own the different elements of the curriculum, assessment, and instruction cycle is to view each of those elements from the perspective of the children in your room. Over the years, I've encouraged teachers to use a simple thought experiment that helps with this very task. It can be used with any of the various responsibilities in the cycle.

As you're planning a lesson or considering instructional approaches, look at your class roster and pick out three children. One child should be your most engaged student in that regard, the one who is most likely to get excited about the activity. The second child should be someone who has often disengaged, wandering aimlessly around the room. Perhaps they sit passively while that sort of activity unfolds. The third child should be someone who, for whatever reason, seems to be activated in unproductive ways. They pump energy not into the planned activity but into some form of behavior that disrupts other children or your teaching team.

Then explicitly walk through the activity while thinking about how each of those children would respond. Of course it's going to be easy to engage the first child, given that you selected them for their engagement! So focus especially on the second and third children. What can you see looking through their eyes? What is it that you could do to engage these children who are so challenging to engage? Are there adjustments you can make before, during, or after the activity to serve them more effectively?

# Assessment Basics in the Early Childhood Classroom

Looking at your classroom through the eyes of the children in it is a powerful way to evaluate the state of the environment you share. A critical additional component of that evaluation is assessment, where you gain knowledge by systematically reviewing each child's development, both individually and in groups.

You are likely to encounter assessments such as environment rating scales, developmental checklists, curriculum-aligned data systems, and so on. Instead of focusing on specific assessments, let's take some time to review the basics of assessment in early childhood education. As noted above, assessments in ECE are typically one of three types:

- **Formative assessment** is used repeatedly throughout the year in order to adjust our teaching to meet the needs of the children we're serving.

- **Summative assessment** is used toward the end of learning cycles to assess our efforts over time and make more substantial adjustments to classroom practice.

- **Informal assessments** are ongoing as we observe students going about their days in our classroom.

Let's start our brief exploration by talking about the foundation for all of these assessments: observation.

## Observation as Foundation

Over the decades, research on human behavior has come to a sobering conclusion about our perceptual abilities. We humans just aren't very good at observing other humans objectively. We tend to sort our impressions based on whether we like someone or not. Our brain picks up positive things from the people we like, throwing away the negative. We see all the faults of people we dislike, ignoring their positive qualities. Our brains are very efficient in these situations. You may recognize this from your most recent argument with your partner, parent, or child!

We need to become aware of these tendencies and replace them with others to develop the skills required for effective observation and assessment. When I teach assessment in teacher training courses, I assign two related homework activities at the start of the semester. First, the students have to go to a public place like a mall or a cafeteria. They identify one or two people and write observations of everything each person does for five minutes, documenting everything they can. Then, the students have to ask someone to observe them for five minutes, silently documenting their behavior as they eat, do their homework, or watch television.

These assignments reveal the problems that unfold whenever one human observes another. Students watching other people eat in a cafeteria, for example, often become very judgmental about people's eating habits. Their observations prompt conversations about the ability to be objective about people's behavior. Some students complain that they ran out of time. So much happened in that five minutes, they couldn't capture it all. To complete the assignment, they needed to ignore certain behaviors; they simply could not track everything that was going on.

Finally, some students always refuse to do the activity. They feel it is unethical for them to observe strangers and write down what they are doing without their permission. Those ethical concerns become even more pronounced with the second assignment, when the observers are now the observed. Students relate their great discomfort knowing someone was watching and documenting their behavior. They regularly demanded the notes from the observers to review whether they were accurate and fair!

In short, these assignments reveal the extent to which observing human beings is fraught with potential inaccuracy, judgment, and ethical problems. (Feel free to take ten minutes and try both of them yourself!) To develop the ability to use assessment tools effectively, I begin with basic training around observation, using the form on page 117.

We use this form to learn how to observe in more appropriate, ethical ways. We aim for observation notes that "SOAR" with these four qualities:

- They should be *specific*, with detail that presents a picture to anyone reading the observation.

- They should be *objective*, judgment-free statements that anyone, not just the current observer, would agree are true.

- They should be *accurate* descriptions of observed behaviors, not observations of inner states or emotions.

# Basic Observation Form

Initials _____

Date _____

Time _____

**Descriptive Notes That SOAR (Specific, Objective, Accurate, Responsible)**

| Judgments | Questions | Brain Chatter |
| --- | --- | --- |
| | | |

- They should be *responsible*, focused only on content agreed upon beforehand and related to the assessment task at hand.

As we've learned, however, our brains will continue to generate content that does not soar! So at the bottom of the form there's space for three categories. The first involves judgments, which you acknowledge and set aside, then get back to observing. Of course, as you observe, questions will arise in your mind: What's happening here? Why did they do that? Children, contexts, and you are changing all the time, so those are valuable components of observation that you want to document and revisit again and again. They will help you see what your evaluative lenses—and perhaps your biases!—focus on.

Finally, there is a space for all the other things that come to mind when you're doing observations. Grocery lists, phone call rewinds, laundry chores—despite your attempts to focus, your brain's going to keep spitting out thoughts no matter what you do! We call this category *brain chatter*. It's where you track the background chatter your brain produces while you're trying to get other work done.

Learning how to observe other people in this more formal way allows you to bring greater skill to all of your assessments, but especially your informal ones. When you notice something happening in your classroom, it's helpful to check your impression and see if it truly *soars*. If it doesn't, you found some aspect of your perception that is a bit biased. Keep an eye out!

# Approaches to Summative Assessment Data

One aspect of early childhood education that can create significant anxiety involves summative assessment data. At specific points during the year, it's likely that you will need to attend a meeting about evaluative data gathered on the children in your classroom. This data could be connected to high-stakes decisions. Funding for your program, quality ratings, and even your job performance appraisal may be based on it. And while it would be great if the data were positive all the time, it's usually a mixed bag, showing areas of strength and areas that need further attention and work.

Most people find these meetings very challenging. It's hard to escape the impression that disappointing data is indication of failure. It seems to obliterate anything positive. But summative assessment data is now a fact of life in our profession. So let's figure out a way to approach that data more positively.

First, it's important to remember the purpose of any data meeting. We review information on the children and program in a spirit of inquiry, reflection, engagement, and innovation to improve our practices. It's about children's learning and growth, and our response to it; good data help us support that learning and growth in ever-more-productive ways.

But any single data report tells only one story. Assessment tools, as I've stressed, cannot possibly perceive the whole child. While data allows us to see multiple perspectives at once, we'll never get the whole picture. Put differently, data is built with tools that are both limited and extremely valuable. Your job is to take full advantage of what's valuable—which of course includes your own perspective!

Here are some useful questions to ask when you're in a summative data meeting.

1. What are some things that you notice about the data? What are the various demographic trends (girls, boys, English speakers, older children, etc.)?

2. Which children are meeting expectations successfully, according to the data? Why might that be?

3. Which children are less successful? Why might that be?

4. Are you surprised by any of the data? Are they reflective of what you see in the classroom?

5. How does this summative data compare to your formative and informal data?

6. What goals or strategies do you want to set to help children further develop?

**TO SPARK YOUR LEARNING...** NAEYC has published many valuable books on powerful assessment practices. *Spotlight on Young Children: Observation and Assessment*, edited by Holly Bohart and Rossella Procopio (2018), dives deep into all aspects of this important topic. *Spotlight on Young Children: Observation and Assessment, Volume 2*, edited by Hilary Seitz (2024), explores new research on assessment and focuses on authentic assessment practices. For teachers new to early childhood, *Basics of Assessment: A Primer for Early Childhood Professionals* by Oralie McAfee, Deborah J. Leong, and Elena Bodrova (2004) is a straightforward, powerful place to start.

# Instruction in the Early Childhood Classroom

There are too many curricular and assessment products available to cover here in any responsible manner. However, over the past decade or two, there has been a tremendous amount of valuable research on instruction in early childhood. What follows are some summaries of the best practices available to you as you implement them in your classroom.

## Embracing Both/And Instruction

In their excellent chapter "Intentional Teaching" in *Developmentally Appropriate Practice in Early Childhood Programs*, Sue Bredekamp and Barbara Willer set the stage by encouraging us to move from either/or to both/and thinking. As Bredekamp and Willer write,

> *Educators plan and implement both teacher-guided and child-guided experiences to help children achieve important learning goals. . . . Children benefit both from engaging in self-initiated, spontaneous play and from teacher-planned and structured activities, projects, and experiences. . . . Children benefit from both opportunities to see connections across content areas through interdisciplinary curriculum and opportunities to engage in focused, in-depth study in a content area. (2021, 8)*

Let's unpack each of these encouragements. Clearly, it's your responsibility to plan experiences and guide children through them. Work with your curriculum guidance and assessment insights to structure beneficial opportunities for children to learn and grow.

But Bredekamp and Willer indicate that your planning should also include opportunities for children to guide themselves, each other, and you through learning experiences. We want children to be able to understand and follow teacher-led instruction but also express their autonomy and initiative regarding their own learning. That means seeking ways to encourage children to participate in the planning of their own learning experiences.

This commitment to children's initiative and autonomy means implementing teacher-planned and structured activities with flexibility and responsiveness. Let's take a math lesson designed for the block area as an example. You've planned a small-group activity to promote an understanding of categorization and sorting. The goal is to have children categorize different block shapes and build small structures using only shapes in a specific category.

Suddenly, you notice that one child has spontaneously decided to combine curved, semicircular blocks with flat rectangular blocks. This creates a more stable structure than they can create with curved blocks alone, which are wobbly building materials. Instead of requiring the child to return to the task you had planned, Bredekamp and Willer would encourage you to see this as an opportunity. The child is taking the initiative to go deeper into the content, exploring features of the blocks beyond categorization to design characteristics. Encouraging that child's initiative can reveal the learning for others in the group as well. But that will happen only if you can pivot to this spontaneous development.

Another important "both/and" involves content instruction. Seasoned teachers develop lesson plans that create experiences for children to engage in focused, in-depth study of specific content. During winter, for example, there may be a weeklong series of lessons devoted to direct instruction about temperature. The lessons center around a science project to create ice in bowls you place outside. That sustained commitment to a set of exploratory questions provides a rich opportunity for children to go deeply into important science concepts. And it's an exciting hands-on opportunity to watch ice freeze and melt.

> We want children to be able to understand and follow teacher-led instruction but also express their autonomy and initiative regarding their own learning.

Bredekamp and Willer encourage you to recognize that these same science concepts occur throughout other planned moments in your classroom. In your art area, children could draw thermometers showing a specific temperature. They could then draw corresponding scenes of what they might do when it's that temperature outside. On a large thermometer you've built for circle time, children can move the "mercury" up and down depending on the day's temperature. And what a great time for children to learn how to make ice cream and describe the different states it goes through from liquid to solid! These interdisciplinary opportunities both deepen children's learning and provide them with multiple ways to access content.

Finally, interdisciplinary opportunities arise from a wide array of instructional approaches. As discussed in chapter 1, many methods not only reinforce direct lessons but enable you to extend content learning through classroom relationships. When a child asks a question, you can expand on any content you've encountered in the room. That means making connections to other discussions and centers, offering additional vocabulary to introduce further nuance, or bringing another child or two into the discussion and posing the question to them. And of course, you can be the one asking open-ended questions that encourage exploration!

Many instructional approaches beyond direct instruction are available to early childhood educators: different forms of play, hands-on activities, verbal explanations, role modeling, art projects that explore drawings and charts, real-world opportunities, online research, reinforcing ideas with books. As you plan, consider all of these and apply the ones that seem most appropriate to the content you present and the children you serve.

As you do so, remember that you learn just like children do. So activate your perseverance and resilience and accept the inevitable mediocre attempts and outright flops as you try out new methods. Give yourself the same grace you give children, allowing for dozens of attempts before expecting yourself to use a new method with mastery.

## Embracing Teachable Moments with Emergent Experiences

Throughout the day, real-world situations provide informal opportunities to reinforce concepts. For example: transitioning from indoors to outdoors and back again; handwashing in warm water before lunch; checking your body's comfort level to determine whether you want to put a sweater on. These opportunities have many different names in early childhood education. They are often called *teachable moments*. They arise suddenly and disappear quickly, providing a moment of entry for responsive, spontaneous teaching. Others refer to these instructional gateways as *emergent experiences*. This phrase emphasizes that the opportunities emerge and can flower into full learning opportunities for children.

It takes practice to notice teachable moments and respond by creating emergent experiences. You can think of this skill as rapid-response developmentally appropriate practice. Using both your observation skills and your understanding of child development, you notice a leap forward in a child's skills or understanding. You embrace it with a corresponding set of supports, encouragements, and opportunities to learn.

> Consider teachable moments and emergent experiences within a serve-and-return framework. Teachable moments are a child's service to you. They are serving their interests and insights into the moment. And creating emergent experiences is your return to them.

Embracing these opportunities may sound complicated at first. However, it's really just a version of the foundation for all early childhood instruction: *serve and return*. In its simplest form, serve and return is the mechanism for language development for children starting at birth. An infant serves to you with a smile or a cry or a gesture. You return that act of communication with one of your own. This continues throughout early childhood in all areas of teaching.

Consider teachable moments and emergent experiences within a serve-and-return framework. Teachable moments are a child's service to you. They are serving their interests and insights into the moment. And creating emergent experiences is your return to them. You take their service and build on it to encourage further engagement.

This approach requires significant instructional flexibility, the magic muscle of all great early childhood educators. They know that there are moments when they need to control the flow and structure of a child's learning experience. But they also know when to let go, step back, and respond. They can hear when the music requires different dance steps from those they had planned. And, like most dancing, it creates a joyous energy that gets other people moving!

# Your Story as a Professional Educator and Caregiver

Review the topics in this chapter. Then grab your journal or a piece of paper and write your answers to these reflection questions:

1. What expertise, knowledge, and insight about curriculum, assessment, and instruction can you bring to children, colleagues, and families as an early childhood professional right now?

2. As you review the chapter, what do you think you need to learn more about to help you serve children better?

3. Are there any challenges you need to confront to better appreciate your curricular materials, understand your assessments and their resulting data, and develop new instructional skills?

4. What learning story do you want to tell about yourself on your journey to become the best educator and caregiver you can be?

# CHAPTER 5

# Family Engagement

A few decades ago, this chapter would have had a different title. We would be talking about "family involvement," not "family engagement." That's because much of the field shared the assumption that the real work of learning and growth happened in school, and families were to be *involved* in that work.

More recently, however, early childhood educators have embraced the term *family engagement*. This term reflects the fact that families provide crucial support and context for young children's growth and development (Bulotsky-Shearer et al. 2012). It's our job to engage families in all that we do, because children's caregivers at home really are vital teaching partners.

For these reasons, we want to engage parents and caregivers as active participants in their children's education. It's not enough for them to be involved. We want them to have power and autonomy as they begin to negotiate school systems with their child. That is to say, we want to engage their energy and support them on the journey of advocating for their children. Often, that journey starts in our early childhood classrooms.

## Foundational Elements for Effective Family Engagement

Of course, many of our foundational principles apply directly to families. We want to make all our interactions with them matter and celebrate their successes, for example. But there are some specific ways that family engagement differs from other classroom practices, requiring some additional guidelines.

*Families and Educators Together: Building Great Relationships That Support Young Children* (Koralek, Nemeth, and Ramsey 2019) provides a rich, detailed overview of family engagement in early childhood programs. The authors share their own foundational elements, characteristics that are in place in schools with strong family engagement practices. While several of their elements stress program-level expectations, others apply directly to your classroom.

There are four important elements that connect to this chapter. These elements of family engagement align directly with the ten principles we've been using. Indeed, the four elements below guide educators to reflect thoughtfully on our values as we create goals and design steps to reach them.

1. **Programs and teachers engage families in ways that are truly reciprocal** (Koralek, Nemeth, and Ramsey 2019, 5). This element reminds us that family engagement is authentic. It is built on human relationships between educators and family members. We seek to meet families where they are, both when things are going smoothly and when things are challenging. Just as we start where children are in our planning, the same is true working with family members. We meet them where they are.

2. **Teachers and programs engage families in two-way communication** (5). This element stresses the importance of open-ended questions, active listening, and respectful responses. That means that one-way newsletters from the classroom to families are a thing of the past! Thanks to recent developments in technology, there are lots of ways to engage families in authentic, back-and-forth communication.

3. **Programs provide learning activities for the home and in the community** (6). Reflecting both what's happening in the classroom and what's happening in children's homes, we do our best to provide appropriate experiences that families can use. These experiences reinforce what's happening in school. They also take advantage of the power of parents and caregivers as children's first teachers, building on their love and commitment to supporting their children's learning and growth.

4. **Programs invite families to participate in decision-making and goal-setting for their child** (5). One key way to collaborate involves setting educational goals for children. We don't just ask for families' reactions to existing goals. Instead, we engage family members in determining their goals for their children and finding ways to incorporate them in our classrooms.

# Family Engagement and Autonomy

Before turning to best practices for family engagement, it's important to acknowledge certain complicating factors you may face. Let's start with a common challenge.

The first four chapters of this book focused on what you can do as an early childhood educator inside a classroom that you largely control. To be sure, there are constraints built into any educational endeavor. No doubt you can list quite a few that apply to your work! But for the most part, throughout each day, you are in charge of determining what happens in your classroom. If you make a decision about something that should be done, you can typically find ways to make that happen using yourself or your team.

In family engagement things are quite different. Consider the basic concept of control. Though you control your own actions, you have no control over what happens in the families of the children you teach. This lack of control can be frustrating at times, especially when families make decisions about their children with which you disagree.

> Accepting that you cannot change families is crucial. But let's be honest: that acceptance can be difficult to maintain! So it's very important for you to develop an ongoing sense of self-awareness as you reflect on your family engagement efforts.

That's when it's valuable to reflect on the times when people had advice for you about things you should do in your family! I'm pretty sure that there were at least a few times when that advice was unwanted or poorly delivered. After all, your autonomy as a family member, parent, or caregiver is important.

That autonomy should be front and center in all family engagement efforts. You ignore it at your peril. Indeed, the very act of trying to impose control on families is a doomed enterprise. What's more, your denial of a family's autonomy is sure to destroy your relationship with those families in the process.

Accepting that you cannot change families is crucial. But let's be honest: that acceptance can be difficult to maintain! So it's very important for you to develop an ongoing sense of self-awareness as you reflect on your family engagement efforts. After all, you want what's best for the children in your care, and that desire can very easily slip into a desire to change a family in ways you think they need. Recognizing that desire when it arises helps you resist acting on it.

# Balancing Family Engagement and Program Realities

The structure of your program also has major implications for building reciprocal relationships with families. Here is a tale from my own experience that illustrates those realities.

For nearly two decades, I worked in programs that required family members to drop off and pick up children in classrooms. That meant that I had two opportunities daily for authentic interactions with the families we served.

Because family members were in the building for arrival and departure every day, everything about our program focused on engagement during those times. Faculty, support staff, and I would all keep our schedules clear so that we could take advantage of these opportunities for interaction. Even families that came and went quickly were there for ten or fifteen minutes a day. That's over an hour per week just for the families who spent the least amount of time in the building! Of course, other families would stay quite a bit longer. This added even more time for informal interactions, sharing perspectives, exchanging ideas, and building trust.

Finding time to give to our family engagement commitments was pretty easy. Then, in 2020, COVID-19 happened.

Suddenly, we needed to completely rethink our arrival and departure routines. We had to prioritize health and safety, not family engagement. That meant teachers met children as they got out of cars in the parking lot and walked them into the school. We had little contact with family members. What contact we did have involved teachers standing outside the cars of family members for impromptu conferences—a lousy substitute for what we had been doing for years.

The amount of time we spent interacting with each family dropped to the bare minimum. We had to cycle dozens of cars safely through a parking lot that wasn't built for the process, and we had to do it quickly. It was rare that any family got more than two or three minutes of attention. Very often families got basically no time at all.

Families also got zero time inside the building. That lack of access created a complicated trust problem. Family members were used to regularly seeing, hearing, and smelling the classroom where their children spent the day. Now that access was completely cut off. That meant that we had to create those missing experiences as best we could, using digital photographs, notes home, and so on.

The pandemic of 2020 was an extraordinary situation, but the differences these two scenarios reveal may be familiar to you. Your school may provide lots of informal and formal opportunities for interaction at arrival and departure. On the other hand, your school may require children to be dropped off at the front door of the building, or perhaps children take a bus to school. These necessary procedures unfortunately eliminate valuable communication opportunities for families. Logistical constraints like these mean that you have to find time to balance family engagement efforts with the realities of your program.

## Balancing Family Engagement and Family Realities

Other factors impact family members' ability to respond to your efforts to engage. Families with adults who stay at home with their children may well have time and energy for family engagement activities and discussions. On the other hand, single-parent families with a working adult are unlikely to have such time and available energy. Meeting families where they are is one of the key components of authentic family engagement. It requires careful attention to the realities of the families you serve.

Paying attention includes using your equity lens to identify who is and is not being truly served by your efforts, regardless of your best intentions. When I was a school director in Oklahoma, I greeted every family every day at arrival and departure if I was in the building. I didn't have to make any effort to connect to the social parents, all fluent in English, who were comfortable chatting with the school director.

But my equity lens revealed that not every family shared those traits. If I wanted to welcome everyone, I had to adjust. In particular, meeting everyone exactly where they were meant that I had to make sure to say hi to people who seemed to be avoiding me! Teenage moms enrolled in the high school across the street; dads struggling with the judicial system; family members behind on required paperwork: those folks usually walked in with their heads down.

They rarely reached out to me, to be sure. But that very fact meant that they were the people I especially wanted to feel welcome and engaged. So I made sure that my daily chats were friendly and positive; that's not the time to jump on someone for missing paperwork! After all, as we know, every interaction matters.

# Designing and Implementing Best Practices for Family Engagement

With these real-world challenges in mind, revisit the four foundational elements named by Koralek, Nemeth, and Ramsey to reflect on your goals and identify steps to reach them. How can you build on those elements as best practices for your own situation?

## Engage Families in Ways That Are Truly Reciprocal

For family engagement to be truly reciprocal, return over and over to principle 3. Be as honest and transparent as possible as you establish and expand your relationships with families. Recognize that such relationships often start with little or no trust, even possibly some distrust. So every interaction you have provides you with an opportunity to build that trust.

When families trust that you are being honest and transparent, they are more likely to respond in kind. Relationships built on honesty and transparency also make it possible for you to understand what families need in order to trust you as a partner in this shared effort. If you don't know who your families are, what strengths they bring to the relationship, and what challenges they face, it's impossible to create truly reciprocal experiences that engage them.

> If you don't know who your families are, what strengths they bring to the relationship, and what challenges they face, it's impossible to create truly reciprocal experiences that engage them.

True reciprocity requires that you use your equity lens. Some families have the resources to give lots of time and energy to family engagement activities you design. Other families can only respond if the opportunities take into account the realities of their lives.

Let's consider a foundational family engagement activity: reading at home. A family with a car, a library card, and lots of books at home can act on your encouragement far more easily than a family with none of those things. In addition, you cannot assume that every adult in the family can read in English. Some may not be able to read in any language. Get to know families and their capacities so you can design opportunities that allow them to reciprocate.

Truly reciprocal family engagement also includes acknowledgement of challenges when things aren't so rosy. Family members want to trust you, but it takes time and effort for you to demonstrate that you are, indeed, trustworthy. After all, they leave the most important person in their lives with you every day! So trust doesn't happen quickly or automatically.

If families have limited access to you, your classroom, or the school, it can be even more challenging. Let's take a look from a parent or caregiver perspective. They don't know what's going on inside a classroom or school each day. Their child isn't yet able to describe in objective detail what's happening. They don't know whether it's quiet or loud, sweet-smelling or stinky! In these situations, it's hard to feel that they have enough information to build that trust.

Strange though it may seem, this scenario is actually a fantastic opportunity to build trust simply by pointing out that it is lacking! It's hard sometimes to say out loud that things aren't the way you would like them to be. But I assure you that acknowledging it is a welcome relief for family members. After all, they are aware that there are trust issues.

Most schools require some form of orientation before children enroll or begin attending. In addition to finding out families' basic characteristics and goals, ask, "What can I do to build and maintain your trust?" Simply asking that question makes it clear that you are paying attention to a remarkably important issue for each family. In addition, the answers you get will help you create truly reciprocal relationships founded on principle 5. This information will give you everything you need to design and plan engagement that works for each family.

Of course, sometimes things go off the rails with a given family. A communication snafu, an unexpected, troubling event . . . any number of things can make a family feel annoyed or even angry. So, when these things happen, your commitment to honesty and transparency will help you move *toward* the annoyed or angry family member. Acknowledge the difficulty and ask them what you can do to rebuild trust. And remember: the fact that they are angry with you, in a strange way, demonstrates that they actually have enough trust to show it to you!

## Engage Families in Two-Way Communication

The examples in the previous section show the benefits of open-ended questions in building strong relationships with families. Such questions are critical invitations for children's learning. They're also critical invitations for adults to help you understand what their family is all about.

"Tell me how you're feeling about the start of the school year." "What does a successful day look like for your child?" "By the end of the year, what sorts of things do you hope your child will know and be able to do?" Every family wants to be asked these questions. The fact that you are asking them in the first place shows a true commitment to building strong communication.

Of course, it's critical that you listen carefully and actively! No two families are the same. And within families, feelings about each child differ as well. So when asking these questions, engage the basics of active listening. Demonstrate your attention with eye contact and nodding; take brief notes; repeat back what you've heard somebody say in an affirming way.

> While one-on-one conversations are the most efficient and effective way to communicate, they're not always possible. That's when to remember that every family wants to be acknowledged personally.

While one-on-one conversations are the most efficient and effective way to communicate, they're not always possible. That's when to remember that every family wants to be acknowledged personally. Brief handwritten notes or text messages to one family are always far more effective than generic newsletters or group blasts to all families. And they can still be very speedy. It usually takes no more than a minute to write a two-sentence note to a family.

If family members can't enter the building or your classroom, help them see what's happening in those spaces. Digital photography and parent communication apps allow you to paint a vivid picture of what a child does each day. When our program started COVID protocols, we made sure every family got at least a few photos or videos of their child every day. Seeing what was happening in the building completely changed the moods of families who were overwhelmed with complicated emotions in the pandemic.

## Provide Learning Activities for the Home and in the Community

Whenever I talk about family engagement activities that promote learning in the home and community, I describe a public service announcement (PSA) I saw on television in the mid-2000s.

> *For the first fifteen seconds, a woman pushes a shopping cart through a grocery store, seemingly by herself. And she seems to be acting very, very strangely in this public community space.*
>
> *Looking in the dairy case, she says, "Mmmmmm. Mmmmm. Milk. Mmmmmmilk." At the meat counter, she chatters away, saying "Ch ch ch ch ch ch ch ch chicken. Chicken." It's pretty odd.*
>
> *In the produce section, she says, "Buh buh buh buh buh buh buh . . ." And then the camera zooms out to reveal a toddler in the grocery cart.*

*The child smiles and bursts out the word, "BANANAS!" Mom leans in and gives the child a kiss on the forehead. The PSA ends with a few seconds about how talking is learning—but by then the viewer already knows that!*

This PSA shows the ideal type of learning activity for home. Let's go through each of its characteristics. How can you make learning activities like this?

*It's free.* Low-cost activities are essential, but free activities are ideal! Often, the families who are most eager to use the opportunities you provide aren't able to spend a lot of money on them. If they could, they might already have purchased such things. Regardless of a family's level of income, having free activities is a real relief. No need to find the money in the budget for this one.

*It requires no additional materials.* Most learning activities for young children involve objects they can manipulate, utensils they can write with, and so on. It may seem that those items are straightforward, but not every family has those things handy. Even if they have them at home, they don't take those objects with them wherever they go. The family in the PSA took nothing extra into that grocery store; they used the materials that were available in the environment. And there are *always* learning materials in the environment if you know how to find them!

*It's equitable.* This materials-free activity is available to everyone. The activity is also adaptable to any family situation. In addition to this PSA in English, I've seen a version in which the mom and child are speaking in Spanish. Mom says "T . . . t . . . t . . . tomate" to the tomatoes and "Lay lay lay lay leche" to the milk. You can imagine the same activity in literally any language, and in many other locations: on city streets, in a park, within the home itself.

*It requires no planning.* The mom in this PSA didn't have to think through a step-by-step plan. That's because this activity is spontaneous, arising from the situation in which the family found itself. It did, however, require understanding. And that's because . . .

*It's developmentally appropriate.* Mom is a great early childhood educator! She understands that her child is developing their phonemic awareness. Walking through the grocery store, she recognizes that they are in a teachable moment. The child knows the names of many items in the store. So she creates an emergent experience for the two of them that targets that developmental goal and provides appropriate scaffolding. And it keeps the child engaged during the family chore. It's brilliant!

*It shows that learning is part of everyday life.* Young children's learning and growth are happening all the time, both with and without intentional adult activity. In this activity, the environment is the most engaging component. Mom takes advantage of the unending string of opportunities that appear in this most ordinary of places. Of course, places that are ordinary to adults are fascinating to young children!

Finally, and most importantly: *The activity is embedded in a joyous, attached relationship between the parent and the child.* Mom knows how to use principle 2 and make every interaction matter. As we know, learning is most productive within strong relationships that activate children's sponge-like neurology. Treating a chore as a fun opportunity for connection brings joy into learning for the child. And what a nice way to get the shopping done for Mom!

As you design learning activities for families, keep the above characteristics in mind. How many of them can you meet?

## Invite Families to Participate in Decision-Making and Goal-Setting for Their Children

In most situations, this foundational element is the trickiest to activate as a best practice. It requires a lot of effort in different areas from both you and each family.

First, it's built on a truly reciprocal, authentic relationship, which takes effort, especially at the start. Second, there is an imbalance related to the different skills and understanding you and the family members bring to the relationship. Family members are unlikely to have extensive training in child development or developmentally appropriate practice. That means that building your relationship with the family will likely include respectful scaffolding of the family's understanding of child development.

This is particularly important as you share how your curriculum, assessment, and instruction support *their child's* development. Of course, you bring expertise in the formal components of early childhood education to the relationship. But family members possess a universe of understanding about their child that is just as important, if not more important.

Let's review the first four components of DAP that we discussed in the previous chapter. We will compare the educator perspective with the family perspective for each component.

1. As a trained early childhood educator, you need to have a comprehensive understanding of child development across several domains. Families have a wide-ranging understanding of their child's development, even if they are not familiar with some components. For example, they might not know the names of the different domains or the research base that supports an area of learning or growth.

2. You need to be able to observe a child objectively, keeping your own biases in check. But family members are not supposed to be objective about their own children! Their parenting biases are grounded in their values and deeply held beliefs about their child.

3. You need to assess a child's knowledge and skills across developmental domains based on the behavior or performance you observed. Family members observe their child in a wider variety of settings than you possibly can. You're largely stuck in your classroom. They are with their child at home, in the community, at family events, and so on. That variety allows them to know how different environments affect their child's skills and understanding with far greater nuance than you. (Remember the story in chapter 1 about Felina who was a cat at school?)

4. You need to review many instructional practices and select the most appropriate one. But you have to provide these instructional practices for multiple children. Family members usually can focus on what works for their particular child with far more time and greater attention.

As you can see, there is plenty of family understanding to use to create a truly reciprocal relationship! But recognizing the ways in which families' knowledge and your knowledge can both be used may require a mindset shift. All too often, educators believe that their expertise is the only one that matters. Some educators believe that certain family members have no expertise at all. But that is a misunderstanding of the foundational research in the field. Failing to recognize the deep expertise in every family is counterproductive. It's also a dehumanizing violation of the principles we embrace.

> The goal is to build a relationship between two experts: you and the family member(s). And one of the great ways to use your expertise is to affirm their own!

The goal is to build a relationship between two experts: you and the family member(s). And one of the great ways to use your expertise is to affirm their own! Starting with open-ended questions about a child's experiences, skills, behavior, and understanding is essential. Family members are filled with fascinating descriptions of their child that you can affirm as important expertise. You can also help them understand how your curriculum and instruction cultivates aspects of their child's development that are important to them. In this way, you are affirming their expertise with your own, valuing both equally. That is true reciprocity!

# Special Topics in Family Engagement

Having created a strong foundation for family engagement efforts, you are likely to encounter some interesting opportunities or challenging situations. Here are some ideas about how you might approach those topics.

## Seeing the Child and the Family in the Classroom

Creating a classroom environment that reflects the children and families you serve is a vital component of early childhood education. Schools are strange places, especially for children who are experiencing them for the first time. Too often, adult family members have bad memories of their own time in school. Anything that you can do to reflect home life can help make transitions easier for children.

For children who are particularly struggling with the transition into school, consider making a small family book. The book can include photographs of family members and of home . . . anything that reminds the child that they have familiar people and places that support them all the time, even when they're at school. These photo books are particularly useful during daily routine transitions and at rest time, so make sure that they are available to children whenever they need them.

Similarly, families who visit your classroom will want to see themselves and their community reflected there. Make a "family wall" where photos and drawings of family members are displayed. Add photographs of community buildings, businesses, and parks. Ask families to add hopes for the year. All of these can be meaningful for family members, either every day at arrival and departure or at special times like open houses.

Items children bring from home present some additional challenges. Representing families and communities in the room takes extra attention when it comes to objects from those places. Aside from personal items such as coats, changes of clothes, and backpacks, nearly all other items accessible to children are available to the whole classroom community. So if you choose to encourage contributions of classroom items from families, be sure to establish a clear approach to sharing those items among everyone in the room. That could be tricky if an item is a prized possession of a single child who tearfully states, "It's MINE!" That item probably should stay at home.

## Family Engagement and Equity

The final note about creating welcoming environments and experiences for families and children requires your equity lens—and this one may be tricky indeed. As a school director, I firmly believed that we had to do our best to make sure that every activity, celebration, or decoration was available to families regardless of income, transportation, language, and so on. While that sounds straightforward to say, it is often challenging to do.

Take open houses. These events are a staple of most educational settings, but a quick review with your equity lens will show that they simply are not accessible for every family. Attendance at open houses requires transportation, time, child care for other children in the family, and language fluency (unless your school provides interpreters). Not every family has all of those things. Those families who are thereby left out are usually the ones who would benefit most from an open house experience. So keep an eye out for who might not be able to attend these important events, and do what you can to provide accommodations. Affirming a family's commitment and sending a handwritten note full of observations, a couple of photographs, and some artwork can go a long way to helping an otherwise marginalized family feel included.

Other common occurrences in early childhood classrooms likely need reexamining. Think of things like holiday decorations that celebrate specific religious or national events. "Dad days" that focus on father-child activities. Even beloved Halloween or pajama days where both children and staff wear costumes. These things regularly fall short when considering all children and families. So it's critical for you to assess how you can be truly inclusive with all families while recognizing the meaningful values of your community.

TO SPARK YOUR LEARNING... You can learn more about how to make thoughtful decisions concerning holidays using the anti-bias materials that have been published by NAEYC. Here's a blog post that provides a good overview of anti-bias from two experts in the field, Louise Derman-Sparks and Julie Olsen Edwards: naeyc.org/resources/blog/anti-bias-and-holidays.

## When Families Are Struggling

Our work with young children and their families means we are often made aware of the challenges that families face. Economic issues, domestic violence, substance abuse, separation, and divorce: the challenges our society faces will, of course, impact children and show up in our classrooms.

When this happens, you need to find a balance between providing useful information and recognizing the limitations of what supports you can offer. For example, your school should include information for families on community resources related to employment, education, housing, food insecurity, and so on. At the same time, we educators have neither the resources nor the training to provide those very services.

One way to provide appropriate support grounded in your expertise involves making "Our Family Now" books. These are developmentally appropriate, classroom-made books. They provide a structured and contained way for children and teachers to acknowledge when family transitions and other challenges are happening. Moving to a new home, the arrival of a new baby, a death in the family: any and all important family events are appropriate for "Our Family Now" books. There are also good published books on the market, but please be sure to read them yourself before using them with a child. The topic might be what you are looking for, but the information or approach might not be.

When you make books yourself, you can focus on the specific situation, event, or context for a specific child. Use simple names and descriptions, with true declarations on each page that can be illustrated and confirmed by the child. Be concrete and specific, free of judgment, morality, and assumptions. The book can be revised and amended by both the child and adults.

An "Our Family Now" book has a very specific format. The first page declares, "I am _____ and this is a book about me." Then the book provides concrete information about the family, home, or situation. Prompts start with "This is my/our _____," and illustrations reflect the child's perspective. Other sentences can explain causality ("When _____ happens, I _____"), family support ("Adults help kids do _____"), and what will and won't change ("Some things won't change. _____ won't change").

"Our Family Now" books balance adult responsibility for the child's safety and well-being with that child's autonomy. This is reflected both in the book's creation and its use. Adults are in charge of building the book itself by prompting language and taking dictation, writing and binding the book, scheduling regular reading each day at appropriate times, and storing the book. And as the situation changes, adults oversee editing and additions to reflect those changes.

Meanwhile, children are given important tasks, with support from family members. Children can draw illustrations or take photographs (with adult guidance) for the pages. With their family members, children can help determine what content needs to be added or revised. And they all answer the key questions that make up the content of the book:

- Who are we? Who is in our family?

- What happened? What's happening? What will happen?

- Where are we? Why are we here?

- What might be obvious to adults but less so to a child?

- What will stay the same? What will change?
- What do we know? What don't we know yet?

Finally, the book doesn't have a neatly wrapped-up ending with a moral lesson. It is merely a description of what's happening, of the reality a child is experiencing. So there's no "everything will be okay" or "soon we'll be happy!" The "now" in "Our Family Now" is critical; no need to jump to false endings.

For two decades, I have seen these books provide support not only for children and their families dealing with a wide range of life situations but also for teachers who are uncertain about how they can support the family. Making the books in partnership with family members is a way of building reciprocal, supportive relationships that help everyone. Usually, the family wants their own copy to bring home and read with the child.

And that's because true family engagement is built on and can reinforce the foundational principles of early childhood education. Simply declaring truths to confirm young children's experiences helps them recognize that adults will take care of them and keep them safe. Children learn that these difficulties are part of life, and that we can talk about them. Providing that language for everyone, simple though it may seem, is truly a gift.

# Your Story as a Professional Educator and Caregiver

Review the topics covered in this chapter. Then grab your journal or a piece of paper and write your answers to these four reflection questions:

1. What expertise, knowledge, and insight about family engagement can you bring to children, colleagues, and families right now?

2. As you review the chapter, what do you think you need to learn more about to help you serve children better?

3. What challenging situations have you encountered? What situations do you anticipate? How might you approach those situations?

4. What learning story do you want to tell about yourself on your journey to become the best educator and caregiver you can be?

# Conclusion

## Continue to Spark Your Own Learning

I hope that *Sparking Learning in Young Children* does, indeed, spark powerful learning for the children in your classroom. I hope that you are able to use this book to design effective plans for those children, both on your own and with colleagues, using child development as a foundation. I hope you build engaging environments that stimulate children's learning and activate tools to gather and use information about that learning. And I hope you partner with families participating in each child's journey.

But *Sparking Learning in Young Children* has tried to energize your learning as well! Activating your own commitment to ongoing learning and growth helps make outstanding early childhood classrooms. Not only do children look forward to such welcoming environments, you and your colleagues benefit from that energy as well.

And that's because our profession requires lifelong learning, not only to support children's development but to maintain our active engagement. Activating our own curiosity and drive connects us to the reasons we chose to work with young children. An early childhood educator who continuously invests in their own learning is also cultivating the mindset to meet each individual child precisely where they are. Time and again, we can rekindle the curiosity and commitment that brought us to the profession in the first place.

For that reason, I hope that you will return to this book when you find yourself challenged by a difficult situation, out of fresh ideas, or simply running on empty. In those moments of transition, I encourage you to return not only to specific chapters but also to the ten principles. Which ones seem particularly important? Are there others that you haven't taken into account? What can you do to activate all of them each day?

Resetting your commitments to the values that underpin early childhood education will help remind you of the reasons that you chose to encounter these challenges in the first place. It's my hope that those principles can refresh your perspective, support a change in mindset, and help you generate some sparks.

Finally, here are a few specific ideas to continue to spark your own learning as an early childhood educator.

## Stay in Touch with the Research

Throughout this book, we've explored recent research and best practices that shape our field. And the research continues! So do your best to stay in touch with that research.

Many organizations publish social media posts or email newsletters. In addition, most state early childhood divisions have resource pages that you can check for updates. Finally, look at publications like *Young Children* and *Teaching Young Children* from NAEYC and *Exchange* magazine from Exchange Press. They are devoted to teacher-centered presentations of recent research and best practices that you can use right away.

## Become Involved in Professional Associations and Advocacy Efforts

Many early childhood associations provide collaboration, support, and training tailored to your community. For decades, I have been involved at both the state and national level with NAEYC, and I have found it to be an enormously valuable space for my professional growth. There are also organizations dedicated to specific communities, like the National Black Child Development Institute, the National Research Center on Hispanic Children & Families, and others.

Professional organizations connect you to valuable information you can use in your classroom. But they also provide collective action opportunities to advocate for the causes that matter to the children and families you serve. Letter-writing campaigns, advocacy visits to your state capital, and similar opportunities are critical elements of leadership development in our field. These groups also help you find partners who share your principled commitment to the field and the children it serves.

## Build Your Systems Understanding

The more you learn about early childhood education, the more you notice the impact of many factors on your classroom. Early childhood education operates within a system. It is important to your leadership development to understand that system. Federal funding streams, state departments promoting quality, school districts, licensing systems, higher education training: these components and others have a huge impact on what we do and how we do it.

Sharon Lynn Kagan and Kristie Kauerz provide an overview of these networks in their book, *Early Childhood Systems: Transforming Early Learning* (2015). Our goal in early childhood education is not only to understand these systems, it is also to help transform them to be as impactful as possible for children and families. For more on effecting transformations, I recommend David Peter Stroh's *Systems Thinking for Social Change* (2015).

In his book, Stroh emphasizes the following key insights to all forms of systems-based change.

- The relationship between problems and their causes is not obvious.

- We unwittingly create our own problems and have significant control or influence in solving them through changing our behavior.

- Most quick fixes have unintended consequences: they make no difference or make matters worse in the long run.

- In order to optimize the whole, we must improve relationships among the parts.

- Only a few key coordinated changes sustained over time will produce large systems change.

These insights can help you act intentionally in the systems that matter to you and your community, and they resonate with the principles in this book. The self-reflection built into several of our principles, especially the equity lens, helps us keep an eye on the unintended consequences Stroh mentions, particularly the ones related to quick fixes. And his emphasis on the relationship between parts reflects our second principle: improved relationships are built on meaningful interactions.

# Find Your Squad

Finally, remember nobody can do it for you, and you can't do it by yourself! That's why it's critical to find your squad. You may be the only early childhood educator in your building. But you are surrounded by hundreds of thousands of other committed educators across the United States.

Dig around in social media platforms for early childhood groups. Research the state and national membership organizations available. Check out podcasts (I'm a fan of Heather Bernt-Santy's *That Early Childhood Nerd* podcast, myself). Even a small amount of effort will help you find like-minded people committed to the early childhood education principles you share. It's a great way to collaborate with others like you, who want to keep sparking their own learning as they spark the learning of young children.

# Appendix A

## The Challenging Behavior Solutions Machine

The Challenging Behavior Solutions Machine was developed to explicitly address the ten principles introduced in this book. This approach helps us lean into principle 5 while collaborating and communicating with lots of honesty, transparency, and trust. Doing so enables us to understand a situation more thoroughly and create a path forward for both the child and the team. The form is on page 145.

Start with spoken reminders about what you can and cannot change (you'll find a framework for this reflection in chapter 2). Then, after introductions and identifying the child or children, describe the challenging, noncompliant behavior in detail. Also describe the situation in which the behavior occurs (time of day, location, and so on). In addition, you need to explicitly name the expectation that the child is violating.

These seemingly simple steps often take several minutes, for at least two reasons. The first is that it's often very hard to describe the behavior without using moral judgments like "wrong" and "bad." So you have to put on your early childhood observation hat. Remember to describe only behaviors with no reference to your assumptions about what a child intends to do, is feeling at the time, and so on. And you have to push past the sorts of generalizations that cloud your understanding. For example, don't fall for the misunderstanding that "they're just trying to get attention." After all, in a classroom that recognizes that education and care are two sides of the same coin, every child deserves and receives plenty of positive attention!

The second reason is that you need to reflect honestly about what precisely is challenging you and your team about the behavior. This can be very tricky indeed. Sometimes it's as straightforward as not following a clearly stated and repeatedly taught rule that disrupts classroom basics—like cubby organization or breakfast cleanup. But often the behavior feels challenging to adults on a more complex, emotional level. Perhaps it makes you feel "disrespected" or "frustrated." Words like that are a clear indication that something more complicated is happening, not just for the child but among the adults.

In quality early childhood classrooms, we remember that adult reactions create an ecosystem within which the behavior exists. That's why the next question, "How are the adults in the room reacting to this behavior?" is so vital. Answering this question takes a lot of trust. When you're feeling frustrated and disrespected, it's hard to open up and speak honestly about what those feelings mean. This is particularly true if you don't feel heard and respected by your administrators or peers. Owning that reactivity, however, is essential. There's simply no way to understand the situation in which the behavior is occurring unless the adults can share how they contribute to that situation.

Next it's time to turn your attention to the positive: the expected behavior that fits the goals and desires of the teaching team. With precise, accurate, and honest detail, the team pieces together a clear description of the expectation that this behavior violates.

Often it's hard to describe the expectation in positive terms. This is particularly the case if a deep sense of frustration makes it difficult for you to recognize the messy situation as a teachable moment. Of course, that usually means that teacher frustration arose because the expectation has not been named and taught. Instead, it floats around unspoken, a mystery to children but "obvious" to adults. It's a recipe for both child and adult reactivity!

Once you have a clear understanding of the behavioral expectation that the adults have, it's time to put on your DAP hat and ask the question, "Is this expectation developmentally appropriate for young children, and for this child in particular?" Very often, this produces a sobering conversation about the developmental limits of preschool children. The team may not have fully recognized those limits.

I have often reached this moment in the process only to learn about a situation that was quite developmentally *inappropriate*. Perhaps we learn that the teacher was giving a child a four-part multistep direction that the child simply was incapable of understanding, retaining, and recalling all the way through the final step. Suddenly, by framing the "challenging behavior" within a child development context, we saw that a child who "never finishes cleaning up" was, instead, put in situations where they were doomed to be unsuccessful. That same child might be perfectly able to do those steps when you scaffold the activity, helping them recall and remember each step at the appropriate time and celebrating success at each step. Suddenly, a child who "never finishes cleaning up" has support to master that very act!

Realizations like this allow you to break expectations down, identify a child's strengths that you can build on, and plan sequential opportunities for all children. This helps them develop the necessary skills you're looking for, with lots of instructional support and time. That's when you answer the final two questions: "How do we teach it? What do the adults need to do to support this learning?" These action steps can only be effective once you can see the full context and complexity of these "challenging behaviors."

# Challenging Behavior Solutions Machine

**1.** Review: What is and is not in our power to change?

**2.** Identify the child(ren).

**3.** Describe the challenging, noncompliant behavior. When and how does it occur?

**4.** How are the adults in the room reacting to this behavior?

**5.** What expectation is the child violating? Be precise, accurate, and honest.

**6.** Is this expectation developmentally appropriate for young children? Explain.

**7.** Is this expectation developmentally appropriate for each specific child? Explain.

*If the answers to 6 and 7 are "yes," then...*

**8.** How do we teach it? What do the adults need to do to support this learning?

# Appendix B

## Building a Strong Teaching Team

As discussed in chapter 2, Emisha Maytubby designed a set of strategies for improving the quality of early childhood teaching teams. Her research demonstrates that improvements help both the collaborating adults and the children they serve.

In her research, Maytubby identified four specific factors that are essential to effective preschool teams.

- Supportiveness: The environment in which people work supports their efforts and is aligned to shared goals. Everyone on the team expresses their desire to share in successes and to identify the strengths of others.

- Openness: Members of the team promote honesty and transparency. They have open conversations when needed to build interpersonal trust.

- Personal style: Colleagues work with others with whom they share similar styles or whom they enjoy working with despite differences in style. Like any interpersonal relationship, the individuals work to make their personal styles mesh effectively.

- Action orientation: Individuals on the team not only are committed to doing the work of the classroom but share responsibilities in a proactive manner and encourage others to do the same.

To promote these characteristics, Maytubby created a reflective process and several forms to facilitate the process. It begins with an initial meeting using the Teaching Teams Reflective Meeting: First Meeting form (page 148). The purpose of this meeting is to help teaching teams have a shared constructive conversation about preferences and styles. Next turn your attention to the Shared Responsibilities Plan (page 150). This planning tool dives into the heart of the specific tasks that teachers perform on a daily basis. It approaches those tasks with an attitude of collaboration and mutual support.

After one month, team members complete the Teaching Team Practices and Perceptions Rating form (page 152) to survey and document practices and perceptions. This form allows each individual the opportunity to reflect on a series of questions that promote the building of interpersonal relationships founded on shared responsibility. It's an important step. While it can be easy to name successes, it's often more difficult for us to address challenges directly.

After each individual fills out the rating form, the team reviews their responses to get a sense of how people scored areas differently. The Teaching Teams Reflective Meeting: One Month Follow Up form (page 154) supports this step. Sometimes you will find that there's general agreement about a strength or a challenge, and those are good to acknowledge. More interesting, however, are the places where items are scored inconsistently. Perhaps one teacher indicated that everything is going fine and another teacher named something as a serious concern. Focus attention on that inconsistency in perceptions. It is almost certainly related to a problem in the interpersonal relationships between those individuals. This review is vital to the process, requiring that everyone be as receptive as possible to the feedback.

Since we can all struggle with giving and receiving feedback, it's important to keep prioritizing the principles. Emphasize positive intent. Move from blame and judgment to ownership. Explicitly commit to doing the best with the team at hand, pointing out strengths. All of these can lead to more conversations and, thus, more trust, building the team as you go.

To support ongoing communication, Maytubby provides two additional meeting forms—one for a quarterly meeting (page 156) and one for a special meeting when challenges are present (page 158).

# Teaching Teams Reflective Meeting: First Meeting

| Lead Teacher (LT): | Date: |
|---|---|
| Assistant Teacher (AT): | |

The purpose of this meeting is to help teaching teams have a shared constructive conversation and share responsibilities. At the beginning of each school year, have each person discuss the following questions.

What are your individual strengths?

LT:

AT:

What do you enjoy most about working with children?

LT:

AT:

Which daily routine or activity do you enjoy doing most with children and why?

LT:

AT:

Which is your least favorite daily routine or activity to do with children and why?

LT:

AT:

How do you like to give and receive feedback?

LT:

AT:

How will you discuss problems when they arise?

LT:

AT:

Describe your view of team teaching.

LT:

AT:

What are some beliefs about classroom management that you feel are nonnegotiable? (e.g., babies sitting in dirty diapers)

LT:

AT:

What do you think are the primary responsibilities of each teacher?

LT:

AT:

| Signature: | Signature: |
| --- | --- |

Next, complete the Shared Responsibilities Plan.

# Shared Responsibilities Plan

| Teaching Team: | Date: |
|---|---|
| **Cleaning Routines** | **Staff Responsible** |
| ✔ Preparing table and materials for breakfast | |
| ✔ Cleaning after meals | |
| ✔ Bathroom routines (*e.g., diapering, brushing teeth*) | |
| ✔ Assisting children with cleaning after activities | |
| ✔ Sanitizing toys | |
| ✔ Complete cleaning chart | |
| **Teaching Responsibilities** | |
| ✔ Preparing materials for circle time | |
| ✔ Facilitating circle time | |
| ✔ Preparing materials for centers | |
| ✔ Recording observational notes | |
| ✔ Preparing materials for small group | |
| ✔ Facilitating small group | |
| ✔ Setting up center materials | |
| ✔ Rotating to centers/interest areas | |
| ✔ Daily attendance | |
| ✔ Daily infant/toddler/two sheets | |
| | |
| | |
| | |

*(left margin, rotated: Daily)*

| | Cleaning/Routines | Staff Responsible |
|---|---|---|
| **Weekly** | ✔ Wash laundry | |
| | | |
| | | |
| | **Teaching Responsibilities** | |
| | ✔ Write lesson plans | |
| | ✔ Review observation notes and enter into database | |
| | ✔ Organize materials for the next week | |
| | ✔ Check out library books | |
| | | |
| | | |
| | | |
| **Monthly** | ✔ Write newsletters | |
| | ✔ Family contact logs | |
| | ✔ Emergency contact update | |
| | ✔ Supply orders | |
| | ✔ Bulletin boards | |
| | | |
| | | |

| Signature: | Signature: |
|---|---|

# Teaching Team Practices and Perceptions Rating

On a scale of 1 to 7 please rate the following statements with 1 being strongly disagree and 7 being strongly agree.

1. I enjoy working as a team with my co-teacher(s).   ① ② ③ ④ ⑤ ⑥ ⑦

2. I feel that my co-teacher(s) and I share responsibilities for all activities in our teaching team.   ① ② ③ ④ ⑤ ⑥ ⑦

3. I find it easy to communicate with my co-teacher(s).   ① ② ③ ④ ⑤ ⑥ ⑦

4. My co-teacher(s) and I incorporate each other's teaching styles into our teaching team.   ① ② ③ ④ ⑤ ⑥ ⑦

5. At least once a week, my co-teacher(s) and I discuss the teaching responsibilities (e.g., decide who will facilitate circle time or small group).   ① ② ③ ④ ⑤ ⑥ ⑦

6. At least once a week, my co-teacher(s) and I discuss how to handle the classroom management as a team (e.g., how to ensure the classroom runs smoothly, prevention of disruptive behavior, and so on).   ① ② ③ ④ ⑤ ⑥ ⑦

7. My co-teacher(s) and I vary the workload so that both of us perform meaningful activities (e.g., we take turns facilitating circle time and performing cleaning tasks).   ① ② ③ ④ ⑤ ⑥ ⑦

8. As a team, my co-teacher(s) and I have sufficient time to communicate.   ① ② ③ ④ ⑤ ⑥ ⑦

9. I address any conflicts with my co-teacher(s) immediately.   ① ② ③ ④ ⑤ ⑥ ⑦

10. My co-teacher(s) and I incorporate each other's strengths into our teaching team.   ① ② ③ ④ ⑤ ⑥ ⑦

11. My co-teacher(s) and I incorporate each other's cultural perspectives or beliefs into our teaching team.
① ② ③ ④ ⑤ ⑥ ⑦

12. My co-teacher(s) and I discuss our curricula at least once a week (e.g., what theme or project to use, which objectives to cover, and so on).
① ② ③ ④ ⑤ ⑥ ⑦

13. My co-teacher(s) and I discuss child assessments as a team at least once a week (e.g., who will observe which child, what objectives will be observed, how to assess, and so on).
① ② ③ ④ ⑤ ⑥ ⑦

14. My co-teacher(s) and I agree as a team on our teaching responsibilities (e.g., who will facilitate circle time).
① ② ③ ④ ⑤ ⑥ ⑦

15. My co-teacher(s) and I agree on how to handle the classroom management.
① ② ③ ④ ⑤ ⑥ ⑦

What works well for your classroom teaching team?

_____
_____
_____
_____
_____
_____
_____

What challenges have you experienced with your co-teacher(s)?

_____
_____
_____
_____
_____
_____
_____

# Teaching Teams Reflective Meeting: One Month Follow Up

| Teaching Team: | Date: |
|---|---|

*Prior to meeting have teachers individually complete the Teaching Team Practices and Perceptions (TTPP) rating and have copies at the meeting. Encourage the staff to be open about their individual responses and assure them that information will be used to build a strong teaching team.*

Opening discussion talking points:

- ✔ Discuss with staff the importance of being open and honest regarding teaching team practices.

- ✔ Remind staff of how each person prefers to receive feedback (from first meeting).

- ✔ Remind the staff that the information is not a personal attack and sometimes it is uncomfortable to hear feedback; it's natural to feel "weird."

Discuss the ratings from the TTPP and ask each teacher:

- ◆ Which set of items did you agree or strongly agree with the most? (e.g., communication, sharing responsibilities, and so on)

- ◆ Which set of items did you disagree or strongly disagree with the most?

Discuss the items that teachers rated differently by more than one or items that were rated as "neutral."

◆ What specific actions in the classroom made you agree or disagree with that item?

Develop a plan for working through any major differences (items that were off by more than one).

◆ What actions need to take place for the team to work better at [write the areas in which the teachers disagree]? (e.g., communication, sharing responsibilities, and so on)

Signature: _____ | Signature: _____

# Teaching Teams Reflective Meeting: Quarterly Follow Up

| Teaching Team: | Date: |
|---|---|

*Prior to meeting have teachers individually complete the Teaching Team Practices and Perceptions (TTPP) rating.*

1. What does your partner do really well?

2. Discuss the changes in the ratings since the last meeting and possible reasons why.

**3.** What are some ways that the team can work better together?

◆ What routines or activities would you like to do more?

◆ What routines or activities would you like to do less?

Signature: _____ | Signature: _____

*Modify the Shared Responsibility Form if needed.*

# Teaching Teams Reflective Meeting: Special Meeting

| Teaching Team: | Date: |
|---|---|

*Use this form when a special meeting is needed for those teaching teams having more challenging issues. It may be best to meet with the teaching team members separately.*

1. What do you feel are the major issues with your teaching team?

2. What strategies have you implemented to resolve the issues?

3. What type of support do you need to resolve the issues?

Develop a plan to provide more support to teaching teams.

| Signature: | Signature *(if needed)*: |
|---|---|

# Appendix C

## Strategies for Meeting Facilitation

As discussed in chapter 2, effectively working with teams requires a wide set of skills, including meeting facilitation. It may be that you do not possess a confident handle on those skills!

Facilitation, like all sorts of other group encounters, requires understanding and buy-in from everyone. It's not just the responsibility of one person to facilitate a meeting. Rather, the group needs to approach a meeting with a sense that leadership is distributed among everyone.

As a result, a great place to start is where we started in this book—with the ten key principles (page 3). By initiating your meetings around a shared set of principles, you set expectations for how each participant in the meeting should engage. Pointing out that every interaction matters; prioritizing honesty, transparency, and trust; leading with collaboration and communication; moving from compliance to ownership: these principles are the bedrock of productive meetings that move your agenda forward.

Of course, it's all in the details! I've found it very useful for the group to return repeatedly to basic frameworks for successful meeting facilitation, reminding us of the sorts of roles and activities that promote effective collaboration. You can find many resources available online to support strong facilitation skills and structures.

I am a particular fan of the approach that Seeds for Change uses. This UK organization emphasizes effective, equitable collaboration by clarifying different tasks and roles and prompting discussion about how your team defines a successfully facilitated meeting. I find that their nonhierarchical approach is what good teams thrive on. Their short guide *Introduction to Facilitating Meetings* can be found at seedsforchange.org.uk/downloads/short_facil.pdf.

Finally, and most importantly, it's critical that the group make these strategies their own. That means first having a discussion about what tools make the most sense and how to use them. Once you've created a structure for your meetings and their facilitation, I suggest you repeat that structure several times to get the hang of it. At the end of each meeting, ask participants to contribute their feedback by offering their observations on what worked well, what didn't work well, and what could possibly be changed. Finally, be sure to schedule quick reviews every half-dozen meetings or so to see how you can improve.

# References

Amirault, Chris, and Christine Snyder. 2020. *Finding Your Way Through Conflict: Strategies for Early Childhood Educators.* Minneapolis, MN: Free Spirit.

Balmès, Thomas, dir. 2010. *Babies.* Documentary film. StudioCanal International.

Banning, Wendy, and Ginny Sullivan. 2010. *Lens on Outdoor Learning.* St. Paul, MN: Redleaf.

Bohart, Holly, and Rossella Procopio. 2018. *Spotlight on Young Children: Observation and Assessment.* Washington, DC: National Association for the Education of Young Children.

Bredekamp, Sue, and Barbara Willer. 2021. "Intentional Teaching." In *Developmentally Appropriate Practice in Early Childhood Programs Serving Children from Birth Through Age 8*, fourth edition, 5–23. Washington, DC: National Association for the Education of Young Children.

Brillante, Pamela. 2017. *The Essentials: Supporting Young Children with Disabilities in the Classroom.* Washington, DC: National Association for the Education of Young Children.

Broderick, Jane Tingle, and Seong Bock Hong. 2020. *From Children's Interests to Children's Thinking: Using a Cycle of Inquiry to Plan Curriculum.* Washington, DC: National Association for the Education of Young Children.

Brown, Brené. 2018. *Dare to Lead: Brave Work. Tough Conversations. Whole Hearts.* New York: Random House.

Bryant, Adam. 2023. "The Leap to Leader." *Harvard Business Review.* July–August 2023. hbr.org/2023/07/the-leap-to-leader.

Bulotsky-Shearer, Rebecca J., Xiaoli Wen, Ann-Marie Faria, Debbie L. Hahs-Vaughn, and Jon Korfmacher. 2012. "National Profiles of Classroom Quality and Family Involvement: A Multilevel Examination of Proximal Influences on Head Start Children's School Readiness." *Early Childhood Research Quarterly* 27 (4): 627–639. doi.org/10.1016/j.ecresq.2012.02.001.

Byington, Teresa A., and YaeBin Kim. 2017. "Promoting Preschoolers' Emergent Writing." *Young Children* 72 (5): 74–82. naeyc.org/resources/pubs/yc/nov2017/emergent-writing.

Bynoe, Nadia Kenisha, and Angelique Thompson. 2023. *The Gift of Playful Learning*. Huntington Beach, CA: Shell Education.

Derman-Sparks, Louise, Debbie LeeKeenan, and John Nimmo. 2023. *Leading Anti-Bias Early Childhood Programs: A Guide to Change, for Change*, second edition. New York: Teachers College Press.

Early Learning Division at the Oregon Department of Education. 2022. "Rules for Certified Child Care Centers." Office of Child Care. oregonearlylearning.com/wp-content/uploads/2017/03/OCC-0084-Rules-for-Certified-Child-Care-Centers-EN.pdf.

Gallo, Amy. 2022. *Getting Along: How to Work with Anyone (Even Difficult People)*. Boston: Harvard Business Review Press.

Greenfield, Daryl B., Alexandra Alexander, and Elizabeth Frechette. 2017. "Unleashing the Power of Science in Early Childhood: A Foundation for High-Quality Interactions and Learning." *Zero to Three* 37 (5): 13–21.

Head Start of Lane County. 2013. "Setting Up the Physical Environment." Updated August 2013. hsolc.org/resources/setting-physical-environment.

Heroman, Cate. 2017. *Making and Tinkering with STEM: Solving Design Challenges with Young Children*. Washington, DC: National Association for the Education of Young Children.

Kagan, Sharon Lynn, and Kristie Kauerz, eds. 2015. *Early Childhood Systems: Transforming Early Learning*. New York: Teachers College Press.

Kethledge, Raymond M., and Michael S. Erwin. 2017. *Lead Yourself First: Inspiring Leadership through Solitude*. New York: Bloomsbury.

Koralek, Derry, Karen Nemeth, and Kelly Ramsey. 2019. *Families and Educators Together: Building Great Relationships That Support Young Children*. Washington, DC: National Association for the Education of Young Children.

McAfee, Oralie, Deborah J. Leong, and Elena Bodrova. 2004. *Basics of Assessment: A Primer for Early Childhood Professionals*. Washington, DC: National Association for the Education of Young Children.

NAEYC. n.d. "The 10 NAEYC Program Standards." Accessed February 29, 2024. naeyc.org/our-work/families/10-naeyc-program-standards.

NAEYC. 2019. "Advancing Equity in Early Childhood Education Position Statement." Accessed February 29, 2024. naeyc.org/resources/position-statements/equity.

NAEYC. 2020. "Core Considerations to Inform Decision Making." Developmentally

Appropriate Practice (DAP) Position Statement. Accessed February 29, 2024. naeyc.org/resources/position-statements/dap/core-considerations.

NAEYC. 2022. *Developmentally Appropriate Practice in Early Childhood Programs Serving Children from Birth Through Age 8,* fourth edition. Washington, DC: National Association for the Education of Young Children.

Novak, Sara. 2023. "Half of the 250 Kids Expelled from Preschool Each Day Are Black Boys." *Scientific American.* January 12, 2023. scientificamerican.com/article/half-of-the-250-kids-expelled-from-preschool-each-day-are-black-boys.

Scott, Kim. 2019. *Radical Candor: Be a Kick-Ass Boss Without Losing Your Humanity,* fully revised and updated edition. New York: St. Martin's Press..

Seitz, Hilary. 2024. *Spotlight on Young Children: Observation and Assessment, Volume 2.* Washington, DC: National Association for the Education of Young Children.

Sinek, Simon. 2011. *Start with Why: How Great Leaders Inspire Everyone to Take Action.* New York: Penguin.

Smith, Jodene L. 2023. *What the Science of Reading Says: Literacy Strategies for Early Childhood.* Huntington Beach, CA: Shell Education.

Stone, Douglas, and Sheila Heen. 2015. *Thanks for the Feedback: The Science and Art of Receiving Feedback Well.* New York: Penguin.

Stroh, David Peter. 2015. *Systems Thinking for Social Change: A Practical Guide to Solving Complex Problems, Avoiding Unintended Consequences, and Achieving Lasting Results.* White River Junction, VT: Chelsea Green.

Terrell, Ann McClain. 2018. *Graceful Leadership in Early Childhood Education.* St. Paul, MN: Redleaf.

Waldinger, Robert, and Marc Schulz. 2023. *The Good Life: Lessons from the World's Longest Scientific Study of Happiness.* New York: Simon and Schuster.

# Index

# C

# About the Author

Chris Amirault, Ph.D., served for two decades as the director of NAEYC-accredited Early Head Start, preschool, and preK programs in Rhode Island and Oklahoma. He was president of the Rhode Island Association for the Education of Young Children and has served as chair of the Council for NAEYC Accreditation, as a member of the NAEYC Affiliate Advisory Council, as a founding facilitator of NAEYC's Diversity and Equity Interest Forum, and on NAEYC working groups for developmentally appropriate practice and equity. Chris has taught undergraduate and graduate courses in early childhood education at Brown University, the Community College of Rhode Island, the University of Oklahoma, and elsewhere and served as director

of the Institute for Elementary and Secondary Education at Brown. Coauthor with Christine M. Snyder of the Free Spirit book *Finding Your Way Through Conflict: Strategies for Early Childhood Educators* (2021), he has published articles in early childhood journals and presented many times at early childhood conferences. Chris has a Ph.D. in cultural studies from the University of Wisconsin-Milwaukee.

# Accessing the Digital Resources

The digital resources provide templates for the forms in this book. The digital resources can be downloaded by following these steps:

1. Go to **www.tcmpub.com/digital**

2. Use the 13-digit ISBN number to redeem the digital resources.

3. Respond to the question using the book.

4. Follow the prompts on the Content Cloud website to sign in or create a new account.

5. The content redeemed will appear on your My Content screen. Click on the product to look through the digital resources. All file resources are available for download. Select files can be previewed, opened, and shared. Any web-based content, such as videos, links, or interactive text, can be viewed and used in the browser but is not available for download.

For questions and assistance with your ISBN redemption, please contact Teacher Created Materials.

**email:** customerservice@tcmpub.com

**phone:** 800-858-7339

www.ingramcontent.com/pod-product-compliance
Lightning Source LLC
Chambersburg PA
CBHW041426120626
46547CB00002B/112